The Religious Right
in Southern Africa

The Religious Right in Southern Africa

Paul Gifford

BAOBAB BOOKS

UNIVERSITY OF ZIMBABWE Publications

Co-published by

Baobab Books
P.O. Box 1559, Harare, Zimbabwe
and
University of Zimbabwe Publications
P.O. Box MP45, Mount Pleasant, Harare, Zimbabwe.

ISBN 0–908311–06–0

The publishers gratefully acknowledge the assistance towards the
publication of this book received from the CWME – Urban Rural
Mission of the World Council of Churches.

Cover design by Maviyane Pike, Harare.

Typeset by University of Zimbabwe Publications.

Printed by Jongwe Printing and Publishing (Pvt) Ltd.,
P.O. Box 5988, Harare.

Contents

Contents

Foreword

Christians are not a homogeneous group. If anything, they represent the whole spectrum of the society from which they have come. This fact cannot be over-emphasized as it reflects the fragmentation of human society.

Southern Africa — a region that has endured the scourge of racism — now requires further scrutiny as the religious divide becomes more pronounced with the advent of sects referred to as the religious right. Though not exclusively Protestant, they come by and large from the fundamentalist stream of the Church.

Victims of oppression and discrimination invariably understand the Christian faith quite differently from these new groups. Their hope lies in the restoration of Justice. The fundamentalists, on the other hand, whilst arguing for the inerrancy of the Bible and for the salvation of souls, show a remarkable selectivity in the emphasis they place on certain teachings of Scripture.

Because most of these groups are of American origin, they reflect the views espoused by the religious right in the United States of America. In order to understand the roots of this fundamentalism, it is essential to know the constituency of the fundamentalists, their beliefs, political expression and activities in society.

Fundamentalists evidently consist of disparate elements which support the evangelical or charismatic thrust. They do, however, operate under a network of carefully co-ordinated and interlocking directorships. What has now come to be known as the New Right consists of people who mainly oppose social care services, who support free enterprise and military expenditure. Fiercely anti-communist, they endorse actions designed to enhance American influence and safeguard American interests. Within their own societies they are members of lobby groups actively engaged in promoting their causes.

Born-again Christians, evangelical alliances, preachers well known through their television work, join hands to propagate their particular brand of faith and 'social' teaching. They disapprove of Christians with strong social consciences, or those who engage in what may be interpreted as political activity. In the process, they give unqualified support to many repressive administrations in different parts of the world. Their posture seems to pay scant attention to issues of justice, and they underscore the unbridled rapacity currently in vogue. Wealth acquired for purely selfish motives seems to become a God-given blessing. Prosperity is the name of the game.

As these beliefs are bound to impinge on us as we interact with them, a real appreciation of the world as it is developing is essential. The Church is not full of innocents, nor exempt from subversion and manipulation.

This book is long overdue and should be read by all. Through the research that has gone into its preparation, it should help clarify our stance, for example when faced with tempting invitations or offers of free trips. This book is a must for all, especially for those who hold important office at all levels in the Church.

+Khotso Makhulu
Co-President of the World Council of Churches
Former President of the All-Africa Conference of Churches
Archbishop of the Church of the Province of Central Africa
Bishop of Botswana

Gaborone, July 1988

viii

Preface

This book examines a recent but important religious phenomenon in Southern Africa — the spread of a particular kind of Christianity. To understand this phenomenon properly, one must begin in the United States, where this kind of Christianity originates. Chapter One of this study, therefore, treats of this Christianity in the United States. Chapter Two examines the role of this Christianity when it moves outside the United States, in particular to Latin America and South Africa. Chapter Three analyses in some detail particular organizations which promote this kind of Christianity in Zimbabwe. In these chapters the treatment is mainly historical and sociological.

In Chapter Four the treatment changes somewhat. This part is more theological, and attempts an evaluation of different kinds of Christianity. I am aware that in this fourth part many points are raised that call for far more extended treatment then is given them. I think all the points raised can be defended; my excuse for not discussing each point exhaustively is that to do so would make this part excessively long and change the balance of the book.

For help of various kinds, I would like to express my gratitude to the following: Prof. Adrian Hastings, University of Leeds; Mr Colin Brown and Dr William Shepard, University of Canterbury, New Zealand; Prof. Herman and Mary Waetjen, San Francisco Theological Seminary; Prof. Charles Villa-Vicencio and Mr Harald Winkler, University of Cape Town; Mr Peter McBurney, University of New South Wales; Prof. Carl-Fredrik Hallencreutz, University of Uppsala; Mr Steve Askin, Harare; Dr Des Gasper, Dr Anthony Chennells, Dr Ephraim Mandivenga, Prof. Lee Snook, Prof. Tim McLoughlin, Miss Sioux Harvey, Miss Véronique Wakerley, and Prof. Ray Roberts, University of Zimbabwe; Ms Deb Preusch and Mr Tom Barry, The Inter-Hemispheric Resource Center, Albuquerque, New Mexico; Mr Hugh Lewin and Miss Irene Staunton of Baobab Books. For his editorial assistance, I owe particular gratitude to Mr Roger Stringer of University of Zimbabwe Publications.

1 The American Religious Right

The New Right is a term coined by Kevin Phillips in 1975 in reference to the 'Coors/Richard Vigurie/New Right complex'. He used the phrase to distinguish this complex or coalition from the network of older groups marching under the flag of conservatism. The United States national media picked up the term from Phillips and it entered common parlance.[1] Thus the term will be used here, with the ready admission that it is a broad term which encompasses all sorts of disparate groups.

The New Right can be traced back to the McCarthy era of cold-war anti-communism, but it was the Goldwater candidacy of 1964 that really created it. After that fiasco, the New Right broke with ordinary conservatives and set out to build its own constituency. The New Rightists looked for more support from Middle America, and they were less concerned with respectability, prepared to incorporate fringe elements like White supremacists, rabid anti-communists and TV preachers. They also tapped the widespread dissatisfaction with big government, big labour, and what was seen as the drift away from the basic values of God, family and country. And after the trauma of Vietnam, and in the face of what they considered Carter's accommodation to the Soviets, they demanded that Uncle Sam flex his muscles and 'Make America Great Again'. By the time of Reagan's candidacy in 1980, the New Right network was in existence to offer widespread public support, a definite political agenda, an ideological framework and material assistance.

For all the apparent novelty, many insist that the distinction between traditional conservatives and the New Right is more a matter of style and

---

[1] P. M. Weyrich, 'Blue collar or blue blood? The New Right compared with the old right', in R. W. Whitaker (ed.), *The New Right Papers* (New York, St Martin's Press, 1982), 49. For the following paragraphs, see especially Weyrich, and also T. Barry, D. Preusch and B. Sims, *The New Right Humanitarians* (Albuquerque, The Inter-Hemispheric Education Resource Center, 1986), 5–11.

appearance than of substance. This may well be so. But whatever their importance, there are novelties. The New Right is clearly less élitist and intellectual. It is determined and — this is certainly new — believes it can win. It has a moral quality of righteousness. It understands the importance of mass organizing, sloganeering, press conferences, media manipulation and public relations.[2]

The New Right embraces a wide variety of groups. Its institutional base is a wide network of think-tanks, lobbying organizations and public pressure groups. The think-tanks generate ideological justification, scholarly analyses and policy alternatives. They also provide recruitment pools for the Reagan administration. Among these think-tanks are older ones like the Hoover Institute, American Enterprise Institute, the Center for Strategic and International Studies, and newer ones such as the Heritage Foundation and the National Strategy Information Center.[3] Lobby groups include military ones like the American Security Council, and the Coalition for Peace through Strength, and others such as the Conservative Caucus. Pressure groups such as the Liberty Foundation and the Eagle Forum perform the vital function of popularizing the New Right's ideology.

Thus there is a sharing of values along with a division of labour according to expertise and spheres of influence. Business élites generate cash; names always mentioned are Joseph Coors, Richard Mellon Scaife, Nelson Bunker Hunt and Patrick Frawley, among others. Academics promote policy. Religious leaders and direct-mail specialists stir up popular support. Thus, with the private sector mobilized, politicians and the military attend to legislation and the implementation of the New Right's programme. All these disparate elements are orchestrated by a fairly small network of interlocking directorships.

What do all these groups have in common? They all oppose social services, advocate capitalism and military spending. Their ideology has been characterized as 'economic libertarianism, social traditionalism, and

[2] For a sketch of present-day US conservatism, divided into traditionalists, libertarians, neoconservatives (mostly refugees from the 'Utopian lunacies' of 1960s liberalism), and the New Right (with both religious and secular versions), see B. Berger and P. L. Berger, 'Our conservatism and theirs', *Commentary* (Oct. 1986), 62–7.

[3] For a good account of the origin, nature and function of think-tanks, and a detailed discussion of four important ones (The American Enterprise Institute, Heritage, the Center for Strategic and International Studies, and Cato), see G. Easterbrook, 'Ideas move nations: How conservative think tanks have helped to transform the forms of political debate', *Atlantic Monthly* (Jan. 1986), CCLVII, vii, 66–80.

militant anti-communism'.[4] This last quality cannot be overemphasized: what seems to hold all these groups together is anti-communism.

Traditional conservatives were originally isolationist. However, during the cold-war anti-communist hysteria, they gave qualified support to the containment and counter-insurgency policies of the Truman, Eisenhower and Kennedy administrations. In the 1960s, though, they felt that both political parties were too accommodating to the 'red menace' and called for a more active defence of the 'free world'. This anti-communism is an uncompromising ideology that holds that there can be no accommodation between East and West. In this view, Russia, having devoured Eastern Europe, is now set on devouring the rest of the world. For the New Right, the world is divided in two: 'theirs' and 'ours'. Theirs is ever expanding, ours is ever threatened. In any conflict, the Soviets must be the hidden enemy. This bi-polar or dualist view of the world conveniently overlooks such phenomena as the Sino-Soviet split, the Non-Aligned Movement, and the internal causes of many countries' revolutionary movements. What has become the most distinctive feature of the New Right's anti-communism is its fight-back strategy. The advances of world communism must be rolled back. Born in the New Right think-tanks, this policy has become known as the 'Reagan doctrine'. Fighting the Soviets is to be done on what is called their own terms, with their own weapons — armed revolutions, psychological operations, destabilization and strategic alliances.

Along with the Reagan doctrine goes the military doctrine of Low Intensity Conflict. Believing that the USA is facing 'total grass-roots war' supported by the Soviet Union for the purposes of undermining democratic and capitalist values in the Third World, yet viewing direct intervention of US troops only as a highly undesirable last resort, the USA must fight this subversion using all available resources — mercenaries, surrogate forces, Pentagon involvement in 'humanitarian assistance' for strategic purposes, private as well as government aid, and a psychological operations campaign within the USA to build support.

To repeat, this counter-revolutionary and interventionist coalition is in no way monolithic. The groups that make up the New Right have all sorts of divides between them. But what seems to hold them together is the common ground of anti-communism.

[4] J. L. Himmelstein, 'The New Right', in R. C. Liebman and R. Wuthnow (eds.), *The New Christian Right: Mobilization and Legitimation* (New York, Aldine, 1983), 15.

Now a crucial part of the New Right's formula of success is its religious component. The New Right borders on a religious movement anyway, with its assumed morality, its ethos of a crusade against godless communism, its belief in its role of defender of freedom, democracy, family, Christian values. But media ministers like Jimmy Swaggart, Pat Robertson, Jerry Falwell, James Robison, Jim Bakker and Tim LaHaye have integrated New Right ideology into their preaching. They bring their message of God, country, capitalism and anti-communism to the masses, providing financial support to the New Right, but, above all, providing a popular base for its agenda.

The religious sector of the New Right is no more monolithic than the New Right itself. It contains many traditional Catholics — Catholic groups like Opus Dei and the Knights of Malta are an integral part of it. However, it is really a development of conservative Protestantism. Here the labels can sometimes become confusing. Most of the religious component of the New Right would call themselves evangelicals, that is, they would insist that the Bible is their one spiritual guide and authority, and that their salvation comes through belief in Jesus Christ and a personal adult conversion experience. It is this direct spiritual 'born again' experience that they would probably regard as the key factor. A third of North American adults consider themselves evangelicals. They still tend to be older, poorer, worse educated, female and living in the South,[5] but the pattern is changing. Evangelicals are a shapeless and diverse group and any generalization about them can be faulted. Fundamentalists are essentially evangelicals whose attitude and behaviour stamp them as more hard-line — thus, 'a fundamentalist is an evangelical who is angry about something'. 'Pentecostals' may hold very similar beliefs, but play down doctrine at the expense of personal experience of gifts like speaking in tongues, healing, and prophecy. 'Charismatics' are low-key pentecostals who remain in the main-line Protestant denominations or even in the Catholic Church.

This evangelical (in the broad sense) brand of Christianity has increased

---

[5] *The Economist* (16 May 1987), 26–7; *Time* (2 Sept. 1985), 40–3; L. Bourgault, 'The "PTL Club" and Protestant viewers: An ethnographic study', *Journal of Communication* (1985), XXXV, 132–48; J. H. Simpson, 'Moral issues and status politics', in Liebman and Wuthnow (eds.), *The New Christian Right*, 192–6; P. G. Horsfield, *Religious Television: The American Experience* (New York, Longman, 1984), 111–25; M. Gardner, 'Giving God a hand', *New York Review of Books* (13 Aug. 1987), 17; F. Fitzgerald, *Cities on a Hill: A Journey through Contemporary American Culture* (London, Picador, 1987), 133–9, 168, 174–5.

since 1965, probably by about 50 per cent. During the same period, the main-line churches, although still numerically far superior, have been decreasing, perhaps by 20 per cent.[6] The evangelicals — fundamentalists, pentecostals and charismatics — make something of a strange coalition. Their origins are very different. Pentecostalism began at the turn of the century and spread among both Blacks and Whites as a lower-class, bi-racial movement, characterized more by religious behaviour than by theology. The fundamentalist movement, by contrast, was basically a reaction of White Protestants against modern biblical study, focused particularly on the issue of evolution. Charismatics in the main-line churches are a development of the 1960s. The groups can sometimes be at loggerheads, too. For instance, the healing, prophesying and speaking in tongues that characterize pentecostals can offend fundamentalists, who tend to the view that those gifts were for the age of the Apostles only.[7] And the anti-Catholic tirades of pentecostal preachers like Jimmy Swaggart do not endear him to Catholic charismatics.

Thus there is no simple definition of the 'new religious right': it is impossible to characterize simply.[8] In the USA, the terms 'fundamentalist' and 'evangelical' are often used interchangeably, and both are used to cover the whole religious coalition, including pentecostals and charismatics. This usage is in many respects unfortunate. In other countries, for example, one cannot simply identify fundamentalism and evangelicalism; James Barr, in Britain, who has written so trenchantly against fundamentalism, insists that he is an evangelical.[9] Evangelicalism, of itself, simply means that brand of Christianity which places its emphasis on an authoritative Bible and on a personal experience of Christ rather than, say, adherence to a Christian community. Even within the USA this usage causes confusion. There are evangelicals who do not adhere to, even positively reject, the political agenda of the religious right. The Washington-based Sojourners, for

[6] *Los Angeles Times* (15 May 1987), 1, 3, 28; *Orange County Register* (8 Feb. 1987), 84; *Time* (2 Sept. 1985), 44. Reasons given for these trends differ: *Orange County Register* (16 May, 1987), C10; D. M. Kelley, 'Why conservative churches are still growing', *Journal for the Scientific Study of Religion* (1978), XVII, 165–72; R. W. Bibby, 'Why conservative churches *really* are growing: Kelley revisited', *Journal for the Scientific Study of Religion* (1978), XVII, 129–37. And within fundamentalist churches, the hard-line factions seem to be becoming stronger, see *Time* (24 June 1985), 45–6.

[7] See *Time* (8 June 1987), 52–5.

[8] This is fully discussed in P. L. Shriver, *The Bible Vote: Religion and the New Right* (New York, Pilgrim Press, 1981), 32–41.

[9] J. Barr, *Escaping from Fundamentalism* (London, SCM, 1984), 156–62.

example, whose writings will be used here, are evangelical critics of the right-wing mix of religion and politics. However, since the usage is common I will follow it here, although reluctantly, and in a way that (it is hoped) will keep confusion to a minimum.

In the strictest historical sense, 'fundamentalists' were those American Protestants who formed a coalition of theologically conservative evangelicals in about 1920 to fight tendencies in Christianity that they labelled 'modernism' or 'liberalism'. The word 'fundamentalist' was coined in 1920 by Curtis Lee Laws, the editor of the Baptist *Watchman-Examiner*. He wrote:

We here and now move that a new word be adopted to describe the men among us who insist that the landmarks shall not be removed . . . We suggest that those who still cling to the great fundamentals and who mean to do battle royal for the fundamentals shall be called 'Fundamentalists'. By that name the editor of the *Watchman-Examiner* is willing to be called.[10]

So, strictly, fundamentalists are those who hold to what they consider the fundamentals, and these are normally said to be five in number, although the list may vary slightly. These five are: the authority of Scripture (explained in terms of 'inerrancy', 'infallibility', or 'plenary inspiration'); the virgin birth of Christ; the substitutionary atonement; the bodily resurrection of Christ; and either His deity or His second coming. At one level, the authority of Scripture is obviously the most important; some others are clearly subordinate. For example, fundamentalists make no use of the virgin birth of Christ: it effectively functions as a test to establish one's attitude to the Bible. If one believes in the virgin birth, one is obviously prepared to believe in an extraordinary event on the basis of the Bible alone. If one does not believe in it, one's position on the question of the inerrancy of Scripture is clear.[11] Thus, Barr describes fundamentalism as a 'constellation of differing positions disposed around the centrality and inerrancy of the Bible'.[12] Marsden agrees: 'Inerrancy . . . was to become the code word for much of

---

[10] 'Convention side lights', *Watchman-Examiner* (1 July 1920), 834. See G. M. Marsden, *Fundamentalism and American Culture: The Shaping of Twentieth-Century Evangelicalism, 1870–1925* (New York, Oxford Univ. Press, 1980), 107, and W. Shepard, ' "Fundamentalism": Christian and Islamic', *Religion* (1987), XVII, 356–7, for this and following paragraphs. *The Fundamentals* were a series of writings issued between 1910 and 1915 in the name of the World's Christian Fundamentals Association, founded in 1909.

[11] See Barr, *Fundamentalism* (London, SCM, 1977), 175–8, and also 25–39.

[12] Ibid., 324.

the fundamentalist movement'.[13] However, Shepard is correct in arguing that biblical inerrancy and some of the other essential points are best viewed as defences for a more basic religious vision and concern:

> This vision takes very seriously the sinfulness of man and his consequent need for supernatural redemption, believes that that redemption has been accomplished by Jesus Christ and is mediated to the individual by personal faith, stresses individual salvation and personal morality, and tends to have a 'low' view of the Church and sacraments. The inerrancy of the Bible is important because it is through the Bible that we know of Christ and what he has accomplished, and anything less than inerrancy seems to call into question the authority of this witness.[14]

All those American Christians who would call themselves evangelicals — although they may be somewhat less strict on some of the five fundamentals, and may tend to be more self-critical and far less confrontational towards 'modernists', and even though they generally reject the label fundamentalist — share this religious vision.[15] Pentecostals and charismatics share it, too, although this may not be so immediately evident, for doctrine is of secondary importance for them. Because all in this coalition share this basic religious vision, the same label can be used for all, be it 'fundamentalist' or 'evangelical'.

A further way of clarifying our picture of this evangelical alliance is to look at the organizations which it has spawned, or the issues it addresses. This evangelical alliance (or fundamentalist–pentecostal–charismatic coalition) comes together in various religious and political pressure groups. Falwell's Moral Majority has the highest profile. Christian Voice is almost as well known. They overlap with many others like the American Life Lobby, the Christian Action Council, the National Political Action Committee (also founded by Falwell), Citizens for the Right to Bear and Keep Arms, Coalition for the First Amendment (headed by James Robison), the Heritage Foundation, Life Amendment Political Action, Stop ERA (the Equal Rights Amendment), the Institute on Religion and Democracy, the Confederation of Associations for the Unity of Societies of the Americas (CAUSA — the political wing of the Moonies), and the World Anti-Communist League.[16]

---

[13] Marsden, *Fundamentalism and American Culture*, 56.
[14] Shepard, ' "Fundamentalism": Christian and Islamic', 356.   [15] Ibid., 370, n.9.
[16] For these and other such groups, see Barry *et al.*, *The New Right Humanitarians*, 31–66; Himmelstein, 'The New Right', 14–15; E. Jorstad, *The Politics of Moralism: The New Christian Right in American Life* (Minneapolis, Augsburg Publishing House, 1981), 76; J. L. Guth, 'The new Christian right', in Liebman and Wuthnow (eds.), *The New Christian Right*, 31–3.

All the groups of the religious right can be said to have a common agenda, without its being implied that every group or individual within it approaches every issue with equal fervour. All find political and religious liberalism and secular humanism the enemies of both God and America. This leads them to adopt a common platform.

On family issues, they are against the following: abortion, the Equal Rights Amendment, Federal interference in public education, homosexuality and gay rights, pornography, and school bussing; they are in favour of the censorship of school texts, classroom prayer and the Laxalt Family Protection Act.

On US domestic issues they are against the following: affirmative action, big government, statehood for the District of Columbia, full employment legislation, government support of corporations in trouble (e.g. Chrysler), gun control, Indian tribal claims to land and water rights, instant voter registration, labour unions, minimum wages, national health insurance, open immigration, Occupational Safety and Health Administration (OSHA), situs picketing, social security; they are in favour of the following: the death penalty, the deregulation of airlines, trucking, etc., tax cuts and western land development.

On international issues, they are against *détente*, the Panama Canal Treaty, the recognition of Red China, SALT negotiations, and trade with the Communist bloc.[17]

Another way of establishing the platform of the religious right is to list the issues which Christian Voice has selected by which to assess the 'Christian morality' of members of Congress. Up to 1981, fourteen votes in the House had been selected as critical moral choices. The crucial votes were: for continued recognition of Taiwan as China's legitimate government; against funds for biological, behavioural and social science research; for voluntary prayer in public schools; for a referendum process by local agencies on regulations by the Education Department; against Community Employment and Training Assistance (CETA) funds for persons named as law violators; for terminating Rhodesian sanctions; for protection of the tax-exempt status of private, religious schools; against abortion funds; for ensuring that no one is denied access to education on account of racial or sexual quotas; for students' attending a school nearest their home; for

[17] Taken from *The New Right* published by the American Jewish Committee, Appendix C, 15, quoted in Jorstad, *The Politics of Moralism*, 76–7.

binding budget levels; for a second measure against abortion funds; and for requiring parental consent before dispensing family-planning services to minors.[18]

Newsweek summarized their stance in this way:

> The concerns of born-again politics are defined by Falwell's agenda for the '80s — a pro-family, pro-life, pro-morality platform that, in a triumph of political packaging, turns out to be considerably more 'anti' than 'pro'. Among other things, Moral Majority — and its evangelical allies — are against abortion, ERA, gay rights, sex education, drugs, pornography, SALT II, the Department of Education and defense cuts. They are for free enterprise, a balanced budget, voluntary prayer in the public schools and a secure Israel.[19]

Time gives a similar list, in quite a full discussion, and *The Economist* gives roughly the same issues, bringing the list up to date by adding support for 'Star Wars' and for anti-communist guerrillas.[20] Falwell himself has drawn up a 'Christian Bill of Rights', which gives an indication of how he sees the issues:

Amendment I: We believe that from the time of conception within the womb, every human has a scriptural right to life upon this earth (Exod. 20: 13; Ps. 139: 13–16).

Amendment II: We believe that every person has the right to pursue any and all scriptural goals that he or she feels are God-directed during that life upon this earth (Prov. 3: 5–6).

Amendment III: We believe that, apart from justified capital punishment, no medical or judicial process should be introduced that would allow the termination of life before its natural or accidental completion (Ps. 31: 15).

Amendment IV: We believe that no traitorous verbal or written attack upon this beloved nation advocating overthrow by force should be permitted by any citizen or alien living within this country (Rom. 13: 1–7).

Amendment V: We believe that all students enrolled in public schools should have the right to voluntary prayer and Bible reading (Josh. 24: 15).

Amendment VI: We believe in the right and responsibility to establish and administer private Christian schools without harassment from local, state or federal government (Deut. 11: 18–21).

Amendment VII: We believe in the right to influence secular professions, including the fields of politics, business, law and medicine, in establishing and maintaining moral principles of Scripture (Prov. 14: 34).

---

[18] Shriver, *The Bible Vote*, 19–20. These 'Report Cards', compiled for each Congressman by Christian Voice and the National Christian Action Coalition, and the 'targeting' of the liberals who score badly, are discussed in Jorstad, *The Politics of Moralism*, 82–90. For D. Balsiger's *Biblical Scorecards*, see below.

[19] *Newsweek* (15 Sept. 1980), 32, cited in Shriver, *The Bible Vote*, 19.

[20] *Time* (2 Sept. 1985), 44–6; *The Economist* (16 May 1987), 30.

Amendment VIII: We believe in the right to expect our national leaders to keep this country morally and militarily strong so that religious freedom and Gospel preaching might continue unhindered (1 Pet. 2: 13–17).

Amendment IX: We believe in the right to receive moral support from all local, state, and federal agencies concerning the traditional family unit, a concept that enjoys both scriptural and historical precedence (Gen. 2: 18–25).

Amendment X: We believe in the right of legally-approved religious organizations to maintain their tax-exempt status, this right being based upon the historical and scriptural concept of church and state separation (Matt. 22: 17–21).[21]

These, then, are the politico-religious issues around which the religious right combine. There is, as well, a particular theological issue which tends to unite this evangelical coalition: dispensationalism.[22] Dispensationalism takes its name from the periods or dispensations into which the Bible and world history are supposedly divided. Dispensationalism was first devised and preached to Americans after the Civil War by John Nelson Darby, an Anglo-Irish sectarian and founder of the Plymouth Brethren. He taught that the last period of history had begun, and that the second coming was to occur at any moment. He believed in a secret 'rapture', when Christians would be swept into the air to meet Jesus, just before a period of terrible tribulation occurred, at the end of which time Jesus would return triumphant with his 'raptured' saints to establish his millennial kingdom. Darby's theories (which, of course, he believed were the teaching of the Bible) took hold in the United States, and the dispensationalist notes in the popular *Scofield Reference Bible* helped to spread and legitimize dispensationalist interpretations of prophecy.

American dispensationalism gives a key role to Russia — and here enters a strictly religious component which corresponds to the anti-communism of the New Right generally. After the 'red scare' of 1919–21, much of America

---

[21] Sent out in direct mail order 16 October 1980, cited in Shriver, *The Bible Vote*, 18–19. Falwell cites a scriptural text for each amendment, to give the impression that his programme is 'biblical'. Such 'proof-texting' is obviously highly suspect, and should not be allowed to obscure the fact that, as Robert McAfee Brown states in his response to Falwell's *Listen America!*, the Bible 'does not even begin to compete with' Milton Friedman, General Lew Walt, Senator Jesse Helms and Brigadier-General Andrew J. Gatsis as chief sources of authority for Falwell's views: see R. McA. Brown, 'Listen, Jerry Falwell!', *Christianity and Crisis* (22 Dec. 1980), 361.

[22] This could more properly be called pre-millennial dispensationalism. The different kinds of millennialism, particularly the distinction between post-millennialism (which was world-affirming, optimistic, socially involved, and prominent in the USA until about 1870) and pre-millennialism need not concern us here; for this, see Marsden, *Fundamentalism and American Culture*, 48–62. For the following paragraphs, see L. Kickham, 'Holy Spirit or Holy Spook?', *Covert Action Information Bulletin* (Spring 1987), 6.

became very anti-communist. Fundamentalists picked up an old idea left over from John Cumming, a British apocalyptic writer during the Crimean War, that Russia was Magog, the prophesied invader of Israel in the last days (Ezek. 38–9); 'Son of Man, set your face toward God, of the land of Magog, the chief prince of Meshek and Tubal, and prophesy against him' (Ezek. 38: 2) is taken as a code in which Magog stands for Russia, Meshek for Moscow, and Tubal for the Soviet province of Tobolsk. In this way, fundamentalists spread the notion that the Soviet Union was an evil empire that had a special mission in the last days.[23]

It should perhaps be noted that there was no necessity for fundamentalism to become so identified with anti-communism; there is no necessary connection between the two. It was its American provenance and a particular mind-set so characteristic of fundamentalists that made American fundamentalism so profoundly anti-communist. Marsden puts this well:

The development of hyper-American patriotic anti-communism is a puzzle and an irony in the history of fundamentalism . . . Perhaps the puzzle can be solved by understanding a type of mentality, or disposition of thought, sometimes associated with fundamentalism. This is the dualistic view that sees conflict everywhere; for example, God versus Satan, which comes to be America versus conspirators.[24]

The same must be said of the strictly pentecostal component of the evangelical alliance. There is no intrinsic link between pentecostalism and anti-communism: many Italian pentecostals vote for the communists, Soviet pentecostals are often quite loyal to their government, and the Eastern-bloc pentecostals are grateful for the religious freedom granted to them for the first time by their communist governments.[25] It is *American* pentecostalism which is anti-communist.

American fundamentalism also came to turn its back on social and political issues. This development, too, seems to owe much to accidental factors. Originally, fundamentalists could be interested in social causes.

---

[23] President Reagan described the Soviet Union as an 'evil empire', and 'the focus of evil in the modern world', in a speech to the National Association of Evangelists in Orlando, Florida, on 8 March 1983. The speech was written by Anthony R. Dolan, 'a true believer in the conservative cause . . . [who] had seen the 1980 Presidential campaign as the final game of the World Series for Western Civilization', B. Woodward, *Veil: The Secret Wars of the CIA, 1981–1987* (London, Simon and Schuster, 1987), 235–6.

[24] Marsden, *Fundamentalism and American Culture*, 210. See his whole discussion, 'Fundamentalism as a political phenomenon', ibid., 206–11.

[25] W. J. Hollenweger, *The Pentecostals* (London, SCM, 1972 [German original, 1969]), 469.

The reaction against social involvement seems to be explicable, in part at least, as a reaction against the 'social gospel' or the socially committed kind of Christianity so common in the 1920s and 1930s in America. In rejecting the social gospel because of its supposed neglect of essential doctrine, fundamentalists or conservative evangelicals tended to reject the social involvement that characterized it. The social gospel was closely wedded to the progressive movement in politics. Vehement rejection of the social gospel seems at least part of the reason for the lack of political or social concern that became characteristic of fundamentalism earlier this century.[26]

Initially, fundamentalists had little effect on mainstream American life. They were ridiculed after the Scopes 'monkey trial' of 1925 in which a teacher was prosecuted for teaching evolution, and were lampooned by influential writers like H. L. Mencken and Sinclair Lewis.[27] They emerged into the wider stream of American life as the USA was entering the panic years of the cold war, with Billy Graham as their spokesman. Apocalyptic dualism appealed to Americans encouraged by their government to see political realities in terms of a stark dualism between communism and anti-communism. Many of them saw the invention of the bomb as the fulfilment of biblical prophecy; it was seen as the means whereby elements would melt in the fiery apocalyptic vision of Revelation. The idea of 'the rapture' comforted many because preachers promised that true Christians would be raptured before this outbreak of nuclear tribulation. Envisaging a great crisis in the Middle East, they held that the Soviet Union would eventually invade Israel, but would be destroyed either by American nuclear weapons or by God's direct intervention. They claimed to see signs of this. Interpreting the fig-tree of Matthew 24: 32ff. as Israel, they saw the establishing of Israel in 1948 as the fulfilment of prophecy, and thus their own as the last generation. Later, they saw the capture of Jerusalem by the Israelis in 1967 as the end of 'the time of the Gentiles' (Luke 21: 24), and thus another portent of the end. At the same time, they interpreted the open disrespect for authority and the drug and counter-culture as predictions of the anti-Christ.

[26] Marsden, *Fundamentalism and American Culture*, 90–3.

[27] Mencken has worthy successors in Martin Amis and Gore Vidal; see M. Amis, 'Too much monkey business: The new evangelical right', and 'Vidal v. Falwell', in M. Amis, *The Moronic Inferno and Other Visits to America* (London, Cape, 1986), 109–19 and 120–4, respectively (essays originally published in *The Observer* in 1980 and 1982, respectively); and G. Vidal, 'Bert and La Belle and Jimmy and God', *New York Review of Books* (29 June 1978), 17–22, and 'Armageddon?' in his *Armageddon? Essays, 1983–1987* (London, Deutsch, 1987), 101–14.

In addition, they were growing increasingly bitter and resentful over the consequences of the Vietnam War, both in Vietnam and in the USA itself. All these factors festered through the 1970s until the religious right was ready to fuse with the New Right itself.[28]

Thus, modern fundamentalist religion is inseparable from recent American history. It is incomprehensible without it. The factors which threw up the New Right also led to present evangelical Christianity. Indeed, evangelical Christianity developed the way it has in order to support and legitimize the aims and ideals of the New Right. The current evangelical dispensationalist Christianity is essentially a civil religion. Of course, it is not a civil religion in the 'hard' sense that Bellah and others have claimed for the United States, namely that American culture and institutions themselves assume a religious significance and elicit a religious response.[29] Obviously, the new religious right claim a strong link specifically with Christianity. But the Christian motifs and symbols on which they draw are selected according to a very definite design. Christianity has been fused into American political and economic considerations. Herberg calls this 'American Culture Religion', a 'fusion of religion [in this case Christianity] with national purpose' that 'passes over into the direct exploitation of religion for economic and political ends'. He continues:

In its crudest form, this identification of religion with national purpose generates a kind of national messianism which sees it as the vocation of America to bring the American Way of Life, compounded almost equally of democracy and free enterprise, to every corner of the globe; in more mitigated versions, it sees God as the champion of America, endorsing American purposes, and sustaining American might.[30]

In this new American religious phenomenon, we find both the crude and

---

[28] For full discussion of the development of the new religious right, see A. Lang, 'The emergence of a phenomenon called the religious right', *CALC Report* [*Unmasking the Religious Right*] (1987), XIII, iii–iv, 29–38; Jorstad, *The Politics of Moralism*, 12–30; Himmelstein, 'The New Right', 18–21; J. L. Kater, *Christians on the Right: The Moral Majority in Perspective* (New York, Seabury Press, 1982), 22–37; Fitzgerald, *Cities on a Hill*, 124–32, 176–93.

[29] Bellah's original 1967 essay, 'Civil religion in America', is reprinted in R. N. Bellah, *Beyond Belief: Essays on Religion in a Post-Traditional World* (New York, Harper and Row, 1976), 168–89; see also R. N. Bellah and P. E. Hammond, *Varieties of Civil Religion* (San Francisco, Harper and Row, 1980).

[30] W. Herberg, *Protestant–Catholic–Jew: An Essay in American Religious Sociology* (New York, Doubleday, rev. edn., 1960), 264. Herberg argues here that Catholic and Jewish immigrants to the USA were tolerated by the established Protestants on the condition that they manifested their commitment to the American way of life. Thus the resulting American religion came to worship not God but the self and the nation.

the mitigated versions. Thus, this Christianity has become the religious component of and justification for American policy. Christianity is seen to demand the American policy in the Middle East, particularly support for Israel. Christianity demands huge armament programmes, support to anti-communist guerrillas, *laissez-faire* economics, and the combatting of anti-American forces everywhere they appear, and everywhere they might appear. This is essentially religion in the service of Uncle Sam.

This anti-communist dispensationalism is a powerful force in the United States. This belief is held by influential people. It appears to have been the driving force behind Colonel Oliver North's crusade, for example. President Reagan himself seems to share these views. He believes that this may be the last generation before a nuclear war destroys the Soviet Union. Reagan sees communism in religious terms, and shares the dispensationalist belief that God will 'fulfil his prophecies about the Middle East'. He has viewed the establishment of the State of Israel in 1948 as the fulfilment of prophecy and as a sign that Armageddon is not far off. He has said, 'It can't be long now. Ezekiel says that fire and brimstone will be rained down upon the enemies of God's people. That must mean that they'll be destroyed by nuclear weapons. They exist now and never did in the past'. He went on to identify the 'enemies of God', the prophesied invader of Israel, as the Soviet Union:

'Ezekiel tells us that Gog [*sic*], the nation that will lead all the powers of darkness against Israel, will come out of the north. Biblical scholars have been saying for generations that Gog must be Russia. What other powerful nation is to the north of Israel? None. But it didn't seem to make sense before the Russian Revolution, when Russia was a Christian country. Now it does, now that Russia has become communistic and atheistic, now that Russia has set itself against God. Now it fits the description of Gog perfectly.[31]

Reagan has also said, 'I believe that communism is another sad, bizarre chapter in human history whose last pages even now are being written'.[32] Former Secretary of Defence, Casper Weinberger, likewise sees current events in terms of end-time prophecies.[33] The desirability of those in control

[31] J. Mills, 'The serious implications of a 1971 conversation with Ronald Reagan', *San Diego Magazine* (Aug. 1985), quoted in L. Kickham, 'The theology of nuclear war', *Covert Action Information Bulletin* (Spring 1987), 14. Mills went on to say that Reagan's coolness to all proposals for nuclear disarmament 'are consistent with his apocalyptic views'.
[32] See Vidal, 'Armageddon?', 111.
[33] 'Washington talk', *New York Times* (23 Aug. 1982), quoted in L. Jones, 'Reagan's religion', *Journal of American Culture* (1985), VIII, 65.

of the American nuclear arsenal regarding the Soviets as God's enemies, nuclear war as inevitable, and the end as nigh, is something that deserves more reflection than it is normally given.[34]

The new religious right identifies God with country. Now there has been a long tradition in America identifying God with the United States. As early as 1864, George S. Phillips wrote his book *The American Republic and Human Liberty Foreshadowed in Scripture*.[35] Cherry has traced this movement in *God's New Israel: Religious Interpretations of American Destiny*.[36] For some years the ubiquitous *Plain Truth* magazine has been spreading this message. *Plain Truth* stems from Ambassador College, Pasadena, California, which is an institution of the Worldwide Church of God. All readers are urged to write for a free book, *The United States and British Commonwealth in Prophecy*, which claims that the United States and the English-speaking (White?) Commonwealth nations, being the ten lost tribes, are the end-time recipients of the divine promises to Israel. The *Plain Truth* is not reluctant to spell out the implications of this. For example, since God promised Abraham that 'his seed shall possess the gates [*sic*] of his enemies' (Gen. 22: 17), the Americans and the British have a divine right to the Suez and Panama Canals. Thus, Carter's move to return the Panama Canal to Panama was against God's will: 'The Panama Canal sea gate is part and parcel of America's God-given birthright, and a necessarily vital ingredient which has ensured and protected her inheritance'.[37] Thus God is said to demand an expansionist American foreign policy.

This identification of God and the United States is axiomatic for the new religious right. At the 'Washington for Jesus' rally of 29 April 1980, 'I love

[34] This issue is treated fully in G. Halsell, *Prophecy and Politics: Militant Evangelists on the Road to Nuclear War* (New York, Lawrence Hill, 1987). For Reagan's apocalyptic views and their implications, see R. Dugger, 'Reagan's Apocalypse Now', *Guardian* (21 Apr. 1984), 19; J. Cameron, 'Reagan's Armageddon insight', *Guardian* (24 Apr. 1984), 10; M. Corner, 'Face to faith', *Guardian* (28 May 1984), 8; Jones, 'Reagan's religion', 59–70; Kickham, 'The theology of nuclear war', 10–14; Gardner, 'Giving God a hand', 23; *Newsweek* (5 Nov. 1984), 57; G. Vidal, 'Armageddon?', 101–4; A. Lang, 'Armageddon theology', *CALC Report* [*Unmasking the Religious Right*] (1987), XIII, iii–iv, 5–17.

[35] See D. Maguire, *The New Subversives: The Anti-Americanism of the Religious Right* (New York, Continuum, 1982), 32–4. In the Civil War, this was narrowed to identifying God with the North, ibid., 97–8.

[36] C. Cherry, *God's New Israel: Religious Interpretations of American Destiny* (Englewood Cliffs, Prentice-Hall, 1974).

[37] *Plain Truth* (Sept.–Oct. 1977), 7. Magazine and book from Ambassador College Press, P. O. Box 111, Pasadena CA 91109, USA. The Church publishes a Zimbabwean edition of *Plain Truth*, available from P. O. Box UA30, Harare.

America and I love Jesus' was repeatedly shouted, by speakers and the crowd antiphonally.[38] The leaders of the religious right leave no room for doubt about this. Jorstad, in his study of Pat Robertson, Jim Bakker, Jerry Falwell and James Robison, writes: 'All [the TV evangelists] unabashedly proclaim America as the most Christian nation on earth, God's instrument to do his will'.[39] Tim LaHaye, founder of the American Coalition for Traditional Values and pillar of the religious right, has written a book entitled *Faith of Our Founding Fathers*. In this he argues that the Founding Fathers were just like present-day 'pro-religious conservatives':[40] he claims that 'Evangelical Protestants are not much different today from what they were in 1787'.[41] The country that they created 'was founded on more biblical principles than any nation in history — the secret to America's greatness'.[42] This nation is a 'miracle nation', because signs of God's special care are evident all through its history. 'What was the purpose of this miracle nation that some call "manifest destiny"?' Primarily, so that God could have 'one nation that would do more to fulfil his basic objectives for this [final] age, to preach the gospel to the ends of the earth, than any other nation in history'.[43] However, over the last fifty years 'secularists', 'humanists', and 'liberals' have attempted to turn the real America from this plan of God and this vision of the Founding Fathers. For example,

for 45 years we have consistently retreated in the face of an inferior Soviet enemy . . . Instead of protecting its citizens and those of our hemisphere from barbarous attacks through the use of the Monroe Doctrine established by our Founding Fathers and our sixth president, we have abandoned millions of Cubans, Nicaraguans and others in Central and South America to the spread of godless communism.[44]

LaHaye claims that the Founding Fathers would even have called for the impeachment of those responsible for this abandonment of the Monroe Doctrine. Thus, according to LaHaye, support for the Contras, say, is the duty of any American who wants to be faithful to the vision of the Founding Fathers and to the will of God for America.[45]

[38] Shriver, *The Bible Vote*, 24–5.
[39] Jorstad, *The Politics of Moralism*, 51.
[40] T. LaHaye, *Faith of Our Founding Fathers* (Brentwood TN, Wolgemuth and Hyatt, 1987), 29.
[41] Ibid., 98.   [42] Ibid., 34.
[43] Ibid., 65.   [44] Ibid., 199.
[45] Many of its critics, of course, insist that the new religious right is opposed to all the principles on which the USA was founded, for example, pluralism, tolerance, respect, rule of law, minority rights, checks upon government; see Maguire, *The New Subversives*; Kater, *Christians on the Right*, 78–81;

Because of the importance of this point — namely, the identification of God's will with their understanding of America's interests — it will be elaborated in some detail with regard to two of the most prominent of the leaders of the new religious right, Jerry Falwell and Pat Robertson.

Falwell was born in 1933 in Lynchburg, Virginia. His father was an ambitious small-businessman who shot and killed his brother in an argument, apparently in self-defence. Remorse and business failure drove him to despair and drink. Falwell was a fairly wild youth, who started studying engineering, but after a conversion experience in his second year, switched to a Baptist Bible college in Missouri. After Bible college he returned to Lynchburg in 1956 to found his own church. With tremendous drive, he increased his church's activities to include a printing press, summer camp, youth ministries, a college (later university), and a television programme, 'The Old-Time Gospel Hour', which, thanks to national distribution, made him well known throughout the country. These enterprises, though dogged with financial irregularities, have continued to expand. Originally, though like many Southern preachers segregationalist and opposed to the civil-rights movement, he expressly repudiated political involvement. However, in 1976 he began a series of 'I Love America' rallies which led him to associate with politicians, and during this period he came into contact with the Washington-based activists of the New Right. Thus he was led step by step into politics, which culminated in his founding of the Moral Majority in 1979. (In 1980 he repudiated as 'false prophecy' a 1965 sermon in which he had expressly denounced Christian involvement in politics.)[46] Falwell insists that God 'established' the USA.[47] Falwell's agenda is clear from his appeal letter of 2 October 1980, entitled 'I'm looking for Flag-Waving Americans!'

Dear Friend,
I am urgently searching for one million Flag-Waving Americans! And I want

Shriver, *The Bible Vote*, 72–9; E. Pell, *The Big Chill* (Boston, Beacon Press, 1984); J. Buchanan, 'Church and State: Anatomy of a relationship', *CALC Report [Unmasking the Religious Right]* (1987), XIII, iii–iv, 18–28. Gore Vidal expresses this characteristically: the founders of the American Republic certainly 'would have regarded the Scofield–Falwell–Reagan sky-god as a totem more suitable for men who walk with their knuckles grazing the greensward than for the upright citizens of the last best hope of earth', 'Armageddon?', 109–10.

[46] See Fitzgerald, *Cities on a Hill*, 143–56, 170–9.

[47] J. Falwell, *Listen, America!* (New York, Doubleday, 1980), 43, cited in Maguire, *The New Subversives*, 33.

them to fly the American Flag in front of their homes or offices on Election Day —
November 4th. Why? Because regardless of who you vote for, I want this nation
to know that Christians are proud of their flag! Will you join me as a Flag-Waving
American? You see, what this country needs is Christians like you, who will get tears
in their eyes when they see 'Old Glory' unfurled. We've had enough *anti-God, anti-
American* flag burning Americans who are disgracing our stars and stripes . . . May
I send you a Flag Kit?[48]

Falwell claims that the free-enterprise system is from God — it is clearly
outlined in the Book of Proverbs.[49] His domestic programme is clear from
his Bill of Rights which we have already seen. For Falwell, it is clear that
liberals, by definition godless and unbiblical, 'cannot hold public office
because liberals are on a path to both atheism and socialism'.[50] And God
is against welfare, because bread should come from work: 'The work ethic
is a biblical principle'.[51] The foreign policy of Reagan's presidency is
divinely sanctioned. Distaste for the Soviet 'Evil Empire' underlies everything.[52] Falwell has only scorn for SALT. The 'give-away' of the Panama
Canal Treaty pains him. He bemoans the 'no-win' way the Vietnam War
was fought.[53] He even advocates an invasion of Cuba. 'I'd volunteer', he
says, 'We're long overdue'.[54] Though anti-Jewish (they are 'spiritually
blind and desperately in need of their Messiah and Saviour'),[55] his dispensationalism leads him to support Israel on all scores: 'Whoever stands
against Israel, stands against God'.[56] He is in no doubt about the participation of God in the 1967 'miraculous six-day war'. It was impossible for
Israel to have won, 'had it not been for the intervention of God Almighty'.[57]
He fervently supports Israel's claim to the West Bank, because God's
granting the Holy Land to the biblical patriarchs (Gen. 15: 18ff.) was
irrevocable. In his denunciations of the Palestine Liberation Organization,

[48] Cited in Shriver, *The Bible Vote*, 20–1. Characteristically, Falwell goes on, 'So won't you please
sit down — right now — and write your check for $50 or more to the Old-Time Gospel Hour? . . . Please
rush your gift of $50 to me immediately so you will get your Flag Kit before election.'
[49] Falwell, *Listen, America!*, 12, cited in Maguire, *The New Subversives*, 14. Falwell's advocacy of
capitalism is discussed in Kater, *Christians on the Right*, 60–3.
[50] Falwell, *Listen, America!*, 60.
[51] Ibid., 63, 66.
[52] Ibid., 98–9; cited in Kater, *Christians on the Right*, 59.
[53] Falwell, *Listen, America!*, 67, 73; cited in Maguire, *The New Subversives*, 99.
[54] J. Falwell, 'The Old-Time Gospel Hour', 3 July 1983, cited in D. Huntington, 'God's saving plan',
Nacla Report on the Americas (Jan.–Feb. 1984), XVIII, 31.
[55] Falwell, *Listen, America!*, 98; cited in Maguire, *The New Subversives*, 61–2.
[56] *Time* (2 Sept. 1985), 52.
[57] Falwell, *Listen, America!*, 97; cited in Maguire, *The New Subversives*, 99.

he repeatedly quotes God's covenant with Abraham: 'I will bless those who bless you, and curse those who curse you' (Gen. 12: 3).[58] In June 1981, when Israel bombed the nuclear reactor in Iraq, Israeli Premier Begin immediately phoned Falwell for support. His unqualified support has brought him Israeli-sponsored tours and decorations.[59] Falwell considers America's arms production too slow — he sees the current rate of arms production as a form of 'unilateral disarmament'.[60] He supports America's nuclear policies; he argued for them in the Oxford Union against New Zealand's Prime Minister, David Lange, whose government had just banned visits by American nuclear warships. Falwell relates nuclear weapons to the second coming of Christ. In his 1983 attack on the nuclear freeze movement, called *Nuclear War and the Second Coming of Christ*, he writes: 'The one brings thoughts of fear, destruction, and death, while the other brings thoughts of joy, hope and life. They almost seem inconsistent with one another. Yet they are indelibly intertwined'.[61] Falwell seems to have modified his 1981 views on the nuclear war with Russia.[62] His prediction of the total destruction of Russia he now limits to Soviet military might[63] — in his interpretation, 83 per cent of the Soviet soldiers.[64] Falwell, like Swaggart and so many other dispensationalists, believes he will be 'raptured' before nuclear war breaks out.

Falwell's religion is clearly American civil religion. As Robert McAfee Brown concludes his response to Falwell's *Listen, America!*:

Listen, Mr Falwell! Call your position an appeal to patriotism. Call it a plea for a male-dominated society. Call it the gospel of free enterprise. Call it an invitation for America to be policeman of the world. Call it a brief for the Pentagon. Call it what you will . . .
But don't call it Christian, in such a way that nobody else can claim the name. Don't call it biblical . . .'[65]

After Falwell, the best known of the US televangelists is Marion Gordon ('Pat') Robertson, whose candidacy for President has been the high point of

[58] *Time* (2 Sept. 1985), 46.
[59] *Orange County Register* (17 May 1987), K3.
[60] Falwell, *Listen, America!*, 114.
[61] Quoted in Kickham, 'The theology of nuclear war', 9.
[62] *Newsweek* (5 Nov. 1984), 57.
[63] Dugger, 'Reagan's Apocalypse Now', 19.
[64] *Newsweek* (5 Nov. 1984), 57.
[65] Brown, 'Listen, Jerry Falwell!', 364.

the politicization of the religious right. Robertson is the best educated of all the 'electronic' preachers. He is the son of a US senator from Virginia, a graduate of Washington and Lee and of Yale Law School, and a former Marine officer.[66] Unlike the fundamentalist Falwell, Robertson is a pentecostal: he devotes much of his TV time to healing, and claims to have diverted hurricanes from his Virginia Beach headquarters by prayer — and three times.[67] His is equally a civil religion. The politics are every bit as evident as the religion — even though all is presented as a Christian programme. This is clear, for example, from a reply when asked about his presidential candidacy: 'I am being urged by tens of thousands of Christian people around the country to be a champion of traditional values, moral values, a conservative fiscal policy and a strong defence'.[68] The American way of life is 'biblical'; capitalism is the

economic system most closely related to the Bible . . . The basis of free enterprise is very biblical. We read in the Old Testament that in the millennial time everyone will sit under his own vine and under his own fig tree on his own property (Mic. 4: 4). There we have an idealized concept of the private ownership of property.[69]

God's will and the supremacy of the United States are one and the same. In a 1988 presidential campaign speech in Iowa, he said, 'God and hard work made America great. Either we return to faith in God or America will slip to second class status . . . behind Germany, Japan and Korea. [With faith] America will always be number one in the world.'[70] Dispensationalism is his driving force, too. The end is nigh: 'I firmly expect to be alive when Jesus Christ comes back to earth', he writes.[71] The establishment of Israel began the count-down to the end; Ezekiel's prophecies are being fulfilled.[72] The Jews are still God's chosen people, so Robertson gives Israel passionate support. The 'Voice of Hope', Robertson's TV station in

---

[66] P. Robertson and J. Buckingham, *Shout It from the Housetops: The Story of the Founder of the Christian Broadcasting Network* (New York, Bridge Publications, 1972).

[67] Gardner, 'Giving God a hand', 22.

[68] *The Observer* (18 May 1986), 12.

[69] P. Robertson, *Answers to Two Hundred of Life's Most Probing Questions* (New York, Nelson, 1984), 194–5.

[70] *The Observer* (14 Feb. 1988), 9.

[71] Robertson, *Answers to Two Hundred of Life's Most Probing Questions*, 154.

[72] P. Robertson with B. Slosser, *The Secret Kingdom: A Promise of Hope and Freedom in a World of Turmoil* (New York, Bantam, 1984), 213–14. Robertson sees all sorts of current events fulfilling biblical prophecies: for example, the EEC in Brussels fulfils Revelation 17: 9–14, ibid., 214.

Lebanon, 'blasts out a steady stream of anti-Arab rhetoric'.[73] Before Christ returns, there will be a time of Great Tribulation. The anti-Christ will take over. No one will be able to buy or sell without the Number of the Beast [666] stamped on a hand or forehead (Rev. 13: 16f.). Robertson sees this being achieved by engrafting a microchip on hand or forehead.[74] He urges the stock-piling of food for these terrible times. (Unlike Falwell, Robertson believes that true Christians will be raptured *after* the Great Tribulation — hence the need for preparation.)[75] The end, or the battle of Armageddon, will be ushered in by a major war, begun by a Soviet attack on Israel.[76] The Soviet Union will be destroyed, either by US nuclear weapons, tools in the hands of an angry God, or (alternatively) by great earthquakes. The destruction of the Soviet Union will take place in his lifetime.[77]

There is no need to discuss others. Bill Bright, Jimmy Swaggart, James Robison, and Jim Bakker (some of whom will be encountered below) hold to a recognizably similar picture. The most popular — in fact, positively breezy — presentation of this brand of Christianity is *The Late Great Planet Earth* by the former Mississippi tugboat captain, Hal Lindsey.[78] Lindsey sees the return of Christ as imminent, and uses the (more than five hundred, he claims) biblical predictions of the event to describe the scene in detail. These predictions include the establishment of Israel (Ezek. 38–40), the return of Jerusalem to Jewish control in 1967 (Zech. 12–14), the alignment of Arab and Black African states against Israel (Ezek. 30: 4f.), the conversion of Africa to communism (Dan. 11: 35–45), the rise of the USSR as the power in the North (Ezek. 38–39), the rise of communist China as the power in the East (Rev. 9), the rise of a new Roman Empire in the form of the EEC (Dan. 7: 17), the movement to a one-world government (Rev. 17: 3ff.), the apostasy of the main-line churches (2 Pet. 2: 1). He gives a detailed picture of World War III. The Russians, with the Arabs and Africans and East Europeans, will attack Israel — Lindsey even gives maps of their campaigns — and God will crush the Russians (with nuclear weapons?). Then the

[73] Gardner, 'Giving God a hand', 23.
[74] Robertson with Slosser, *The Secret Kingdom*, 215; Robertson, *Answers to Two Hundred of Life's Most Probing Questions*, 157–8.
[75] Robertson, *Answers to Two Hundred of Life's Most Probing Questions*, 155–6.
[76] Ibid., 216.
[77] Speech to the Full Gospel Businessmen's Fellowship International at the 28th Annual World Convention in Philadelphia, 1981, quoted in Kickham, 'Holy Spirit or Holy Spook?', 6.
[78] H. Lindsey with C. C. Carlson, *The Late Great Planet Earth* (New York, Bantam, 1970).

Chinese will fight the West, with the West led by a new Roman dictator. There will be almost total world-wide destruction, but before complete annihilation Christ will return in glory. Lindsey positively looks forward to World War III, the necessary prelude to the second coming. It is hard not to agree with one critic that this second coming is seen as a 'ruthless and colossal right-wing purge'; the good will dwell in paradise, but the good will include no homosexuals, Jews, liberals, socialists, Catholics, few poor and fewer Blacks.[79] It is tempting to dismiss a book like Lindsey's out of hand — a 'farrago of nonsense', Barr calls it[80] — but it has sold over twenty million copies since 1970, and was the best-selling non-fiction book in the USA between 1970 and 1980. The total sales of all Lindsey's books are nearly three times that figure. Moreover, Lindsey claims to have lectured at the Pentagon . . .[81]

For the sake of completeness, a word should be said about two developments that along with the dispensationalism and Americanism distinguish this brand of Christianity. First, there is a strong emphasis on authority in many but not all of these churches.[82] Many of these churches have been influenced by what is called the 'shepherding' or 'discipling' movement, usually said to have begun in the late 1960s. The Fort Lauderdale Five, along with Pastor Juan Carlos Ortiz, an Assemblies of God pastor in California, and Paul Yonggi Cho, pastor of Yoido Full Gospel Central Church in Seoul, South Korea, seem to have been the key influences in this movement.[83] Churches affected by this movement are distinguished by a cell network, in which everyone is answerable to someone higher up in both spiritual and temporal affairs.[84] Biblical texts dealing with authority are given particular emphasis. 'Submission' and its correlative 'taking authority over' are key concepts in this movement. Thus, sociologically, it is interesting that in the last twenty years Christianity has been characterized by two contrary tendencies. In the main-line churches, authority has lost much of its importance; for example, the Catholic Church, traditionally the most

[79] Maguire, *The New Subversives*, 101.
[80] Barr, *Fundamentalism*, 206. Barr's book is a magisterial exposure of the academic pretensions of fundamentalism's supposed 'scholars'. See also Barr, 'The problem of fundamentalism today', in J. Barr (ed.), *Explorations in Theology*, 7 (London, SCM, 1980), 65–90.
[81] *Newsweek* (5 Nov. 1984), 57.
[82] See *International Herald Tribune* (23 June 1986), 2.
[83] S. Diamond, 'Shepherding', *Covert Action Information Bulletin* (Spring 1987), 18–19.
[84] The 500 000 members of Paul Yonggi Cho's church are divided into more than 50 000 cell groups.

authoritarian of all, is now marked by a cheerful readiness on the part of members of good standing to disagree with many points that the Pope and bishops consider essential.[85] On the other hand, these discipling churches have taken almost complete control over members' lives. Sociologically, it can be noted that authoritarianism invariably accompanies apocalyptic thinking. That is how it works; obscure but binding texts necessarily require an élite who can interpret for the masses. This bears out the point often made by Barr, that in practice fundamentalism is far more authoritarian than those churches with ostensibly more authoritarian structures. The theory of fundamentalism is that Scripture determines all church life, and all facets of leadership; in practice, it does not work out so simply. One of the most striking features of fundamentalism is the prominence of human authority.

The ideological leaders or *gurus* of fundamentalism have much greater influence in their constituency than have bishops, theologians or biblical scholars in non-fundamentalist Christianity. Their power to declare and mould the meaning of Scripture is tremendous. But they retain this power only so long as they continue to profess devotion to biblical infallibility and allegiance to the partisan evangelical cause . . . In these ways fundamentalism, in spite of its profession of submission to Scripture, actually uses that profession to maintain the human authority of the group consciousness and its leaders.[86]

Secondly, the last twenty years have seen the diffusion of the so-called 'gospel of prosperity', openly preached by Oral Roberts, Kenneth Hagin, Jim and Tammy Bakker, Kenneth and Gloria Copeland, Robert Schuller, and less openly by many others.[87] This gospel holds that material prosperity is the right of every true Christian. Claiming to build on texts such as Deuteronomy 28–30, Mark 4, and John 3: 16, its advocates insist that anything spent in the Lord's service will bring a rich return; this is called the 'law of increase', or the 'law of sowing'. A rather crude expression of this gospel of prosperity is found in Gloria Copeland's comment on Mark 10: 30f. ('Truly, there is no one . . . who will not receive a hundredfold now in this time . . .'):

You give $1 for the Gospel's sake and $100 belongs to you. You give $10 and

---

[85] See polls published in *Time* (7 Sept. 1987), 80.

[86] J. Barr, 'The fundamentalist understanding of Scripture', in H. Küng and J. Moltmann (eds.), *Conflicting Ways of Interpreting the Bible* (Edinburgh, T. & T. Clark, *Concilium* 138, No. 8, 1980), 73, and see Barr, 'The problem of fundamentalism today', 80–1. For Falwell's 'dictatorial' authority, see Fitzgerald, *Cities on a Hill*, 156–7.

[87] *The Economist* (16 May 1987), 29–30; *Time* (3 Aug. 1987), 58; Gardner, 'Giving God a hand', 17.

receive $1000. Give $1000 and receive $100,000. I know that you can multiply, but I want you to see it in black and white.

Give one airplane and receive one hundred times the value of the airplane. Give one car and the return would furnish you a lifetime of cars. In short, Mark 10: 30 is a very good deal.[88]

Kenneth Hagin, founder of Tulsa's Rhema Bible Church, and indirectly the founder of the Rhema Churches in Southern Africa, has actually said that for a pastor or anyone to drive a Chevrolet instead of a luxury car 'isn't being humble; that's being ignorant' of God's law of prosperity that works for everyone, saint or sinner.[89] By no means all of the religious right subscribe to this. The animosity of Jimmy Swaggart for the Bakkers is partly attributed to their preaching this gospel.[90] At the same time, the appeal of the high-living Bakkers, with their Rolls, gold-plated bathroom fixtures and fifty-foot walk-in closets,[91] lies partly in their embodying the prosperity so many humbler viewers aspire to.[92] The diffusion of the gospel of prosperity can be explained by the astronomical financial requirements of the media evangelists;[93] the promise of huge returns has been successful in persuading followers to meet these bills. It can also be explained as a means of assuaging the consciences of Americans who are becoming aware of the poverty of so much of the world; any brand of Christianity that insists that wealth is not something to be guilty about but, on the contrary, is to be enjoyed as God-given, has considerable appeal. In as much as it diverts attention from the present economic system and merely fosters the determination to be among those who benefit from it, this gospel of prosperity is the polar opposite of liberation theology.

[88] Cited in D. Hunt, *Beyond Seduction: A Return to Biblical Christianity* (Eugene OR, Harvest House, 1987), 66.

[89] Ibid., 65.

[90] See *Los Angeles Times* (15 May 1987), 13, 28; *Orange County Register* (19 Apr. 1987), A11; *Newsweek* (6 Apr. 1987), 30–3; *Time* (6 Apr. 1987), 50.

[91] *Time* (8 June 1987), 52–5.

[92] *Time* (4 May 1987), 40; *Newsweek* (8 June 1987), 42–3.

[93] *Newsweek* (6 Apr. 1987), 32–3; *Time* (6 Apr. 1987), 51. Hence reports that the whole Bakker scandal was a take-over bid by Falwell's rival TV group in the face of a market becoming saturated; see *Newsweek* (6 Apr. 1987), 28–34; *The Economist* (28 Mar. 1987), 41–2; *Newsweek* (1 June 1987), 50–1; *Newsweek* (8 June 1987), 45. For Falwell's costs, see Fitzgerald, *Cities on a Hill*, 150–6.

2 Outside the United States

The American religious right, with its entire political agenda, has spread far beyond the United States. Here the problem of terminology immediately arises in an even more acute form. If within the USA the term 'evangelical' is used rather unfortunately to describe the religious right, its use outside the USA is just as unfortunate and confusing. In Latin America, Christianity has its own special character. For historical reasons, it is overwhelmingly Catholic. The traditional Protestant churches do exist there, but their numbers are small. The churches called 'evangelical' tend to be quite recent, and also tend to have close links with the USA. There is some possibility, then, that they share some of the political and social preoccupations of US evangelicalism.[1] In Southern Africa, however, the Christian landscape is far more diverse. Many evangelical churches have been in the region for decades. Their links with American evangelicalism may be quite loose. There are groups in Southern Africa who describe themselves as evangelical who positively reject the socio-political agenda of the religious right. The most noteworthy is the group of mainly Black 'Concerned Evangelicals' who, in 1986, produced their *Evangelical Witness in South Africa: A Critique of Evangelical Theology and Practice by Evangelicals Themselves*. This remarkable document frequently admits the evangelical tendency to acquiesce in injustice: 'We wish to confess that our evangelical family has a track record of supporting and legitimating oppressive regimes here and elsewhere'.[2] They give reasons: 'Most evangelical groupings with

[1] In discussing Latin America, Valderrey, adapting a typology of Lalive d'Epinay, distinguishes a) 'Historical or Traditional Protestantism', b) 'Fundamentalist or Sanctification Protestantism', and c) 'Sectarian Protestantism'. It is within this third category that he places the religious transnationals like World Vision, Campus Crusade, PTL Television, the Billy Graham Evangelist Association, and Pat Robertson's 700 Club; see his whole discussion, J. Valderrey, 'Sects in Central America', *Pro Mundi Vita Bulletin* (1985), C, i, 4–12, and the editorial note on page 39.

[2] *Evangelical Witness in South Africa: A Critique of Evangelical Theology and Practice by Evangelicals Themselves* (Dobsonville, South Africa, 'Concerned Evangelicals', 1986), 4.

their narrow view of life and their fundamentalistic approach to the Bible, tend to uncritically support existing oppressive systems'.[3] However, they positively repudiate this tendency: 'This tendency of conservatism of evangelicals . . . is a tendency which ends up more on the side of the devil rather than on the side of our Lord Jesus Christ'.[4] They proceed to advocate a radical departure from their past performance, arguing from their evangelical perspective. They go on to attack the American religious right in general and some American evangelists by name. These 'Concerned Evangelicals' illustrate most eloquently that there are Southern African evangelicals who oppose the American religious right. If in Southern Africa the term 'evangelical' is frequently used in its American sense to refer to Christians subscribing to the whole agenda of the religious right, it must be borne in mind that not every South African Christian described as evangelical is necessarily of this stamp.

When one turns to consider the rise of the religious right outside the United States, it is evident that there are four areas where this evangelical revival has been particularly pronounced. These areas are Latin America, the Philippines, South Korea and Southern Africa. Now it is true that, at one level, the explanation of this revival is natural enough. In a recent Vatican document, *Report on Sects, Cults and New Religious Movements*, compiled from reports from all around the world, there is a section entitled 'Reasons for the spread of these movements and groups'. The document notes that crisis situations or general vulnerability can reveal or produce needs and aspirations which lead people to such groups. Some of these needs and aspirations which appear to be met by sects are well discussed under such headings as: the quest for belonging; the search for answers; the search for wholeness, for cultural identity; the need to be recognized; the need for spiritual guidance, for vision, for participation and involvement; the search for transcendence.[5] It is obvious that in all four areas just mentioned there is massive cultural dislocation and serious social and political crises, so one could expect evidence of a revival which might seem to meet these needs and aspirations.

However, one should be alert to the fact that other factors as well could

---

[3] Ibid., 15.   [4] Ibid., 26.
[5] Secretariat for Promoting Christian Unity, *Report on Sects, Cults and New Religious Movements* (Vatican City, The Secretariat, 1986).

lie behind this upsurge of American evangelicalism. For American interests are at stake here, as many parties in the United States are well aware. The last thirty years have seen great changes in religious thinking. In Latin America particularly, the 1960s were a time of considerable reappraisal for the Catholic Church, culminating in the 1968 Medellin Conference, when the Latin American Catholic Bishops declared their option for the poor and committed the Catholic Church to the struggle for justice for the oppressed. That kind of Christianity offers a serious threat to those with vested interests in the old order. For those so threatened, the older pietistic, apolitical Christianity is far preferable. In Latin America particularly, it has become very obvious that Christianity can take either of two very different forms. It can include within its concerns the structures of society, and can commit itself to changing unjust structures where they exist, as liberation theology tries to do. On the other hand, however, it can retreat to a privatized, personal, other-worldly piety which provides little threat to any unjust status quo. Those with vested interests in the old order can see that, in their own interests, they must oppose and discredit the first kind of Christianity, and foster the second.

Such intentions can be found in important American statements. The fifty-three-page policy proposal entitled *A New Inter-American Policy for the Eighties*, issued in May 1980 by the Council for Inter-American Security, advocated what has come to be called the 'Reagan doctrine' of rolling back Soviet gains. The authors wrote: 'Containment of the Soviet Union is not enough. *Détente* is dead. Survival demands a new US foreign policy. America must seize the initiative or perish. For World War III is almost over'. They state unequivocally — if somewhat arrogantly — that 'Latin America, like Western Europe and Japan, is part of America's power base'. They speak quite plainly:

US foreign policy must begin to counter (not react against) liberation theology as it is utilized in Latin America by the 'liberation theology' clergy. The role of the Church in Latin America is vital to the concept of political freedom. Unfortunately, Marxist-Leninist forces have utilized the Church as a political weapon against private property and productive capitalism by infiltrating the religious community with ideas that are less Christian than communist . . .

They also argue that human rights in Latin America are not the concern of the United States; US security interests are what matter. They expressly call for the repudiation of President Carter's policy of attempting to link US aid for Latin American countries to the human rights record of the recipients. 'Human rights, which is a culturally and politically relative concept . . . must be abandoned and replaced by a non-interventionist [!] policy of political and ethical realism.'[6] The five authors of this 'Santa Fe Document' — Lynn Francis Bouchey, David C. Jordan, Lieutenant General Gordon Sumner Jr., Roger Fontaine and Lewis Tambs — were all well known on the boards of various conservative lobbies and foundations around Washington, and the last three all came to have positions in Reagan's administration. This policy document came to be regarded in Central America as the blueprint for the Reagan administration's intentions in the area.[7]

There seems to be evidence that this thinking has been implemented. Penny Lernoux has described the 'Banzer' Plan, 'hatched in the Bolivian Interior Ministry in early 1975 and named for Hugo Banzer, Bolivia's right-wing military dictator. [The plan] was discussed at length in the Interior Ministry, a publicly acknowledged subsidiary of the CIA, after the Bolivian Church began to make trouble for the government by denouncing the massacre of the miners'.[8] The programme attacked, in the words of a Bolivian government memo, 'only the Church's progressive sector . . . not the Church as an institution or the bishops as a group'. The tactic was to 'insistently repeat that they preach armed struggle, that they are linked with international communism, and that they were sent to Bolivia with the sole purpose of moving the Church towards communism'.[9] Among the methods recommended to discredit Catholic progressives was the planting of subversive documents on Church premises. 'The Banzer Plan was later adopted

[6] Committee of Santa Fe, *A New Inter-American Policy for the Eighties* (Washington, Council for Inter-American Security, 1980), 1, 4, 20. See also J. Didion, 'Washington in Miami', *New York Review of Books* (16 July 1987), 22; and M. Elliott, 'Politics in mission', *Accent* (May 1987), 12–13. Valderrey claims that this thinking can be found earlier. He claims that Nixon's Rockefeller Report, written just after the Latin American Catholic Bishops' meeting at Medellin, stated that 'the Catholic Church has ceased to be an ally in whom the United States can have confidence', and recommended — among other things — an extensive campaign with the aim of propagating Protestant churches and conservative sects in Latin America; see Valderrey, 'Sects in Central America', 20. However, I have been unable to find evidence for Valderrey's assertion in the Rockefeller Report: 'Quality of Life in the Americas: Report of a Presidential Mission for the Western Hemisphere', *Department of State Bulletin* (8 Dec. 1969), LXI, 493–540.

[7] Didion, 'Washington in Miami', 22.

[8] P. Lernoux, *Cry of the People: The Struggle for Human Rights in Latin America: The Catholic Church in Conflict with US Policy* (New York, Penguin, 2nd edn., 1982), 142.

[9] Cited in G. MacEoin and N. Riley, *Puebla: A Church Being Born* (New York, Paulist Press, 1980), 50.

by ten governments belonging to the Latin American Anti-Communist Confederation, including Chile, Brazil and Honduras'.[10]

Lernoux gives several examples of the CIA's involvement in Latin America, supporting religious groups which favoured the status quo, and (either themselves or by proxy) discrediting Church bodies struggling for human rights. The CIA 'funded and directed local religious groups in Latin America for all manner of covert activities, from bombing church buildings to overthrowing constitutionally elected governments'.[11] In Colombia, they funded a Church radio literacy programme. In Ecuador, they financed the Social Christian Party, and were involved in labour unions. In Chile, they funded the 'Congress for Cultural Liberty', and funded *El Mercurio*, Santiago's largest newspaper, the news agency Orbe Latinoamericano, the anti-liberationist Centro Bellarmino of Belgian Jesuit Roger Vekemans, and the Catholic movement 'Tradition, Family, Property' (TFP): 'TFP's activities in Chile, Brazil and elsewhere are an important part of the CIA story in Latin America, because its members were the intellectual and financial backers of military coups supported by the Agency'.[12]

So official American bodies like the CIA can certainly manipulate the religious situation to their advantage. One witness before the US Senate Intelligence Committee testified that the CIA had actually staged a campaign in Cuba promoting the second coming of Christ, with dire consequences predicted for Fidel Castro.[13] But one misunderstands the true picture if one looks for CIA manipulation everywhere,[14] for with the advent

[10] Lernoux, *Cry of the People*, 147; see also 142–7 and 59.

[11] Ibid., 288.

[12] Ibid., 295. For further instances of the CIA's manipulation of religious groups, see P. Agee, *Inside the Company: CIA Diary* (New York, Bantam, 1976), 140, 156, 163, 183–4, 223, 229, 231, 236, 285; and also Lewis's comment, 'I never met a Bolivian who did not regard the Summer Institute of Linguistics as the base for CIA operations in Bolivia, possibly in South America itself', N. Lewis, *The Missionaries* (London, Secker, 1988), 108. The Summer Institute of Linguistics (also known as the Wycliffe Bible Translators) is a particularly aggressive US fundamentalist sect.

[13] See F. Landis, 'CIA media operations in Chile, Jamaica and Nicaragua', *Covert Action Information Bulletin* (Mar. 1982), 41.

[14] 'It is as easy and simplistic to say that the increase in the sects in Central America is the result of planned ideological infiltration on the part of US imperialism as it is to ignore the infiltration completely', Valderrey, 'Sects in Central America', 19. Note that the CIA balked at channelling funds to Archbishop Bravo of Nicaragua for fear of compromising him; see Woodward, *Veil*, 374–5. Woodward's book is a chilling description of the CIA out of control, even before the Reagan years. He notes, for instance, that the key to the coup which overthrew Allende was Nixon's friendship with Donald Kendall, chairman of Pepsi Cola: 'The anti-Allende operation was essentially a business decision; Kendall and other US firms didn't want a Marxist leader in Chile. Helms [CIA Director, 1966–73] and the CIA had been misused . . .', ibid., 56.

of Admiral Poindexter and Colonel North and the 'privatization' of American foreign policy, the US government has been able to enlist all sorts of organizations and individuals as surrogates in their 'anti-communist' crusade. These private individuals and organizations give willing and enthusiastic material and financial support to all sorts of 'humanitarian' causes. This support is orchestrated by shadowy figures — like Colonel Oliver North — who can so arrange things that, in Nicaragua, for example, considerable private aid flows to the very areas where the Contras have their bases, thus providing critical economic support for the rebels and their families. Thus, any distinction between US government, military, business, private, institutional and religious activity can become quite artificial.[15] Pat Robertson, for example, provides material assistance to central America with 'Operation Blessing'. His assistance, however, is not just 'humanitarian'; it is part of a larger strategy. He provides the Contras with chaplains and Bibles,[16] and has been filmed reviewing Contra troops.[17] Indeed, his promise of more than a billion dollars to help Rios Montt's Guatemalan junta (1982–3), although the figure was never reached, is regarded as the inspiration for the entire private Contra aid network.[18]

So the New Right organizations combine in all sorts of ways to engineer social and political results in Latin America. The religious right, encouraged to see everything in terms of God versus Satan (effectively, the USA versus the Soviet Union), are in the forefront of this. The aftermath of Nicaragua's revolution furnishes a good example of how religious groups are used in political and social manipulation.[19] A sizeable sector of the evangelical community supported, and still supports, the Sandinista revolution. Four months after Somoza's overthrow in 1979, five hundred evangelical pastors and leaders issued a declaration endorsing the Sandinista government, and encouraging Christian participation in the Sandinista Defence Committees and the literacy crusade. The General

---

[15] This whole area is fully discussed in Barry et al., *The New Right Humanitarians*. For the privatization of US foreign policy, see Woodward, *Veil*, 350, 405, 430, 470.

[16] Robertson's press conference at the National Religious Broadcasters' convention in Washington DC, 4 February 1986, cited by Kickham, 'Holy Spirit or Holy Spook', 4 n.3.

[17] Cover, *Covert Action Information Bulletin* (Spring 1987).

[18] Diamond, 'Shepherding', 24–5.

[19] The following is taken from Huntington, 'God's saving plan', 27–30. Conor Cruise O'Brien provides a particularly perceptive discussion of the religious component in the Sandinista revolution; see C. C. O'Brien, 'God and man in Nicaragua', *Atlantic Monthly* (Aug. 1986), CCLVIII, ii, 50–72.

Assembly of the Evangelical Committee for Aid and Development (CE-PAD) — which includes all the major pentecostal churches among its thirty-seven denominations — issued a pastoral letter in March 1980 stating that they saw 'signs of the Kingdom of God in the Nicaraguan people's efforts to construct a state of life which is dignified and human'. In 1982, CEPAD sent a letter to American Christians urging them to intercede against the 'intolerant and arrogant attitudes of the government of the US against Nicaragua'. So examples of evangelical support for the revolution were evident. However, not all evangelical leaders were happy with the revolution — some had left before or at the Sandinista victory, some were gaoled for war crimes, and nearly all the North American denominations withdrew their missionaries, about a hundred in all. The evangelicals who stayed and who oppose the Sandinistas have registered their opposition in various ways: setting up schemes in opposition to the government; publicly interpreting floods as God's disapproval of the communism of the government; preaching rejection of ration cards because they were a sign of the apocalyptic Beast. (Some even declared that the Sandinista acronym FSLN meant 666, another sign of the Beast.) More significantly, since the revolution there has been a tremendous influx of small new religious sects, directed by evangelists from Mexico, Puerto Rico, Panama and the Southern United States. Some are distant off-shoots of US denominations; others are small itinerant bands with names like 'Church of the Living Waters', 'Divine Call', and 'Midnight Messengers'. These have promoted a stronger expression of 'other-worldly' pietistic spirituality. Many observers see this growth and shout 'CIA'. In the light of Lernoux's evidence, as we have seen, this is not a facile charge.

But, whatever the origin of their money and strategy, several of these evangelical groups have been helping to destabilize the Nicaraguan government. Their activities include channelling undeclared funds to conservative Nicaraguan preachers and producing educational materials that spread anti-communist fear. Each month the Director of Evangelism in Depth (INDEF) has received a personal cheque from 'a North American citizen', on behalf of a US agency which has never revealed its identity. At the request of this North American citizen, the director launders this money and smuggles it into Nicaragua. This money is broken down for 'salary support' for a carefully screened list of pastors. As one programme administrator said, it is 'only for those who are loyal to the Word, loyal to God', unlike 'those who have gotten involved in Nicaraguan politics'. Six hundred pastors — about 40 per cent of all the fifteen hundred active in Nicaragua — participate in this 'salary support programme'. This provides a 50 per cent boost for their salaries. Since their salaries are, not surprisingly, fairly low, these funds constitute a considerable inducement to remain (or become) 'theologically and politically acceptable'. Some of these pastors also join a network designed to 'assist their theological education' through pamphlets and seminars. These seminars can cover themes like Satan's work through the Nicaraguan government and liberation theology, and models of church persecution. Again, for fairly uneducated pastors, such educational opportunities are hard to resist. These pastoral education and orientation programmes are a particularly apt way of political manipulation, given the pastor's pivotal role in a local community. There is evidence of similar activities in all the Central American countries.[20]

Put simply, there are two brands of Christianity evident in Latin America, and they have very different social, economic and political consequences. Dominguez describes them in this way. First, evangelicalism:

> Evangelical doctrine ... saw believers as a body apart from society. They were the only Christians; everybody else, unless saved, was doomed to eternal perdition. Evangelicals' responsibility to society extended no further than to bring the message of salvation. Except for obeying constituted authority, they should have no role in politics. This made them a valuable, if passive, prop for the existing social order. Within their churches, where they found joy, comfort and encouragement to improve their lives, they could experience the 'anticipation of the Kingdom of God'. Outside lay the 'iniquitous world', the 'cess-pool of sin', that regardless of human efforts could only grow worse until the day of Christ's glorious return.[21]

Secondly, the Christianity of liberation theology:

> For radicalized Catholics, salvation referred not only to the hereafter but to life on earth; it was an existential and collective concern, not an individual one. The Gospel had to be understood from the perspective of the poor; the 'Good News' was the message of liberation from all sin, personal and social, and to proclaim the

[20] Huntington, 'God's saving plan', 23–36. US policy in Central America has been widely debated, both for and against, in the *New York Review of Books* during 1986 and 1987. It is also discussed in O'Brien, 'God and man in Nicaragua', and S. Rushdie, *The Jaguar Smile: A Nicaraguan Journey* (London, Picador, 1987).

[21] E. Dominguez, 'The great commission', *Nacla Report on the Americas* (Jan.–Feb. 1984), XVIII, 19. The doctrine of this sector of Christianity is also discussed in Valderrey, 'Sects in Central America', 30–2.

Gospel meant joining with the poor to achieve liberation, transforming the course of history in accordance with God's will.[22]

Of course, not all groups within the Catholic Church support this second approach. But at Medellin (1968) and Puebla (1979) the Latin American Catholic bishops committed themselves to it. It is not only a Catholic agenda: the Latin American Council of Churches has committed itself to it — as has the World Council of Churches. Likewise, not every pentecostal sect or evangelical church has committed itself to the first approach; but many have. And in direct opposition to the doctrinal position of the Catholic Church, of the WCC and the Latin American Council of Churches, evangelicals in Panama in 1982 set up their own Latin America Evangelical Fraternity (CONELA), with founding members like Morris Cerullo,[23] Marcelion Ortiz, and Luis Palau,[24] expressly to promote just this agenda. This brand of Christianity is a decisive vote for the status quo. 'To the dominant sectors it [offers] minimal reproach for their own rapaciousness. Among their workers it [promotes] passive acceptance of authority and the status quo'.[25] Valderrey puts this bluntly:

There can be no doubt that the pentecostal groups (and above all their umbrella organizations), and to an even greater extent the fundamentalists, are related to the most conservative groups within North America and that they constitute a major ideological–religious bulwark of an unjust social order. If in an earlier period it was Liberal Protestantism [which provided the religious justification for American

[22] Dominguez, 'The great commission', 20.
[23] Since 1982, Morris Cerullo World Evangelism has had an office at 34 Wyvern Avenue, Harare. The local director is responsible for Cerullo's ministry in ten sub-Saharan African countries. Among the activities that the office offers within Zimbabwe is a mass-circulation free correspondence Bible course, in both English and Shona. In mid-1988, 1 847 were enrolled for the English course, 457 for the Shona. Cerullo himself visited Zimbabwe from 10 to 16 February 1985, giving a five-day 'School of Ministry' to 1 200 people (including 150 from Tanzania and 50 from Zambia) and a 'Miracle Crusade' at Rufaro Stadium, Harare.
[24] Palau visited New Zealand for a crusade in March 1987. Four Anglican bishops in the North Island were led to issue a pastoral letter in May 1986 explaining why they could not support the crusade. Among other things, they refer to Palau's American influence, apocalypticism, failure to challenge oppressive systems, and his appeal to fame and success. The World Council of Churches has reproduced this pastoral in its *Monthly Letter on Evangelism* (10 Oct. 1986) [available from Box 66, 150 Route de Ferney, CH 1211, Geneva 20, Switzerland]. Raymond Pelly, former Principal of the Anglican–Methodist Theological College in New Zealand, in a fierce criticism of the crusade, wrote: 'It cannot be said too strongly that this is not the Gospel of Jesus Christ, even though the words 'Jesus' and 'Christ' are being used *ad nauseam*. It could be summed up as an amalgam of people's neurotic fears and the militarism and capitalism of Reagan's America'; see R. Pelly, 'Not the Gospel of Christ', *Accent* (May 1987), 9.
[25] D. Huntington, 'The prophet motive', *Nacla Report on the Americas* (Jan.–Feb. 1984), XVIII, 9.

involvement], today it is fundamentalist sectarianism which bears responsibility for the ongoing exploitation, hunger and death in the republics of Central America.[26]

On the question of South Africa, the New Right — as could be expected — has taken a very positive line. They have adopted a very pro-Pretoria propaganda offensive. The main theses are the following: that apartheid has already been largely dismantled because pass laws are gone and mixed marriage is permitted; that the West is manifesting a 'death wish' by facilitating the ANC's eventual seizure of power in South Africa; that the Soviets are building a military base in Southern Africa, and Soviet operatives in the Western media are distorting the facts; that South Africa's State of Emergency has restored order; that the Zulus, led by Chief Gatsha Buthelezi, represent the true interests of South Africa's Blacks and, therefore, should be armed against the 'terrorists'; that the South African government will survive economic sanctions, but thousands of Black workers will be displaced; and that the ANC is not a true liberation movement.[27]

The religious right is in the thick of this propaganda offensive. All these themes are included in David W. Balsiger's *Family Protection Scoreboard* of 1987. Balsiger is a member of the Steering Committee of the Coalition on Revival, and finances various 'freedom revolutions' in Nicaragua, Angola, Mozambique and Afghanistan, but what might give a better indication of his basic orientation and attitudes is the fact that he is the founder and president of the Restore A More Benevolent World Order Coalition — the RAMBO Coalition.[28] He also publishes the *Presidential Biblical Scoreboard* and *The Candidates' Biblical Scoreboard* which give the President's and every Congressman's voting record, judged against so-called 'biblical criteria'. For example, according to Balsiger, Matthew 20: 1–16 — the parable of the landowner who paid the labourers in his vineyard as he saw fit: 'Am I not allowed to do what I choose with what belongs to me?' (Matt. 20: 15) — shows that the Bible opposes the Equal Rights Amendment.[29] Thus, any politician supporting this has gone against God —

[26] Valderrey, 'Sects in Central America', 22, and see also 31, 34; G. Baum, *Religion and Alienation* (New York, Paulist Press, 1975), 209, makes the same point.

[27] Diamond, 'Shepherding', 22 n.34.

[28] M. O'Brien, 'The Christian underground', *Covert Action Information Bulletin* (Spring 1987), 32–3.

[29] Discussed in *Orange County Register* (17 Sept. 1986), A22. For Christian Voice's grading of politicians on their 'Christianity', see Buchanan, 'Church and State', 22–5.

also according to Balsiger, who therefore tells voters so that they can mobilize against such politicians. The whole 1987 edition of the *Family Protection Scoreboard* is devoted to the question of South Africa. It contains articles with the following titles: 'The Marxist Assault' (pp. 6–7), with a boxed article headed 'Africa: the Kremlin's Playground'; 'Apartheid: Its History and Dismantling' (pp. 8–10); 'South Africa: Nation of Strong Religious Values' (pp. 12–14), which includes a section entitled 'Violence Related Activities of the S.A. Council of Churches'; 'Strategic Importance of South Africa' (pp. 15–17); 'American Companies: A Force in Ending Apartheid' (pp. 18–21) — by investment, of course, not disinvestment; 'The Immorality of Disinvestment' (p. 31); 'Disinvestment Movement in the US — A Proven Soviet Active Measure' (pp. 52–3); 'South Africa's Advances in Housing, Health and Education' (pp. 22–3); 'Marxist Violence in the Black Townships' (pp. 24–7); 'Sanctions — Black Leaders Speak Out' (p. 32), which comprises anti-sanctions quotations from such 'elected black leaders' as President Lennox Sebe of Ciskei, Prime Minister George Matanzima of Transkei, and Chief Minister S. S. Skosana of KwaNdebele; 'Mandela — Freedom Fighter or Terrorist?' (pp. 33–7), which, not surprisingly, concludes that Mandela is a terrorist; 'The Celebrity Leaders' (pp. 34–6), which is an attack on Tutu, Naudé and Boesak; 'Dangerous Foes to the North' (pp. 38–9) and 'African Liberation Movements Gone Sour' (pp. 50–1), which bemoan the state of Africa to the north; and, finally, 'How Congress Voted on South Africa' (p. 44).[30]

The article entitled 'South Africa: A Nation of Strong Religious Values' is worth more detailed consideration. The author writes:

From its inception, South Africa has been a nation of strong Judeo-Christian values ... South Africans of all population groups place great importance on prayer and the scripture ... Governmental and civic meetings are opened with prayer ...[31]

South Africa is strong on family–moral concerns. In the area of traditional family values, South Africa puts America to shame. Abortion is still illegal in South Africa ... There are no ERA debates, and secular humanism has only gained a toe-hold in some of the English-speaking universities. Parochial schools are not harassed. Instead, the government subsidizes many Christian schools. South African courts are strong on victims' rights and have a record of handing down stiff

---

[30] All Balsiger's *Biblical Scoreboards* are available from P. O. Box 10428, Costa Mesa CA 92627, USA.
[31] R. Hunsicker, 'South Africa: Nation of strong religious values', *Family Protection Scoreboard* (1987), 13 [availability as in previous footnote].

penalties to criminals . . . Could *Playboy* or *Hustler* sell on South Africa's news-stands? Assuredly not.[32]

Then, as one would expect, comes the inevitable distinction between 'so-called' but perverted Christianity and the true kind. First, the discrediting of liberation theology:

Religious activist leaders [Tutu, Boesak, Naudé, Hurley are mentioned by name] who embrace 'liberation theology' say Christianity calls for a Marxist–Leninist oriented political change to overthrow the present government by any means including violence.[33]

Then comes a list of 'true' Christian organizations which are involved in the evangelical revival sweeping the country. Here are mentioned Africa Enterprise, Campus Crusade for Christ, Full Gospel Businessmen's Fellow-ship International, Youth With A Mission, Samaritan's Purse, and Bible Pathways Ministries. The revival fostered by such organizations is praised uncritically: 'Once again, as in the founding of the Republic of South Africa, religion is playing a central role in sustaining South Africans and strength-ening the country'.[34] Those last few words make the author's agenda perfectly clear, for there is no doubt about which South Africans are being 'sustained' and whose country is being 'strengthened'.

The current Christian right media treatment of South Africa was organ-ized at the February 1986 convention of the National Religious Broadcasters (NRB). At that time the executive committee of the NRB agreed to help a group of White South African pastors form a South African NRB and to support their efforts by touring the country and returning with 'the true story'. Since May 1986 the Full Gospel Businessmen's Fellowship Inter-national has organized tours, with reduced airfares provided by the South African government airline, SAA. To promote the tours, the airline has produced a 30-minute video, 'The Other South Africa', featuring interviews with well-known fundamentalist leaders, including Kenneth Copeland and Ray McCauley, urging Christians to visit South Africa and imbibe its physical and spiritual beauty.[35]

And the 'Christian' media have spread this 'gospel'. Jerry Falwell, after his August 1985 visit to South Africa, during which he spent six hours with Foreign Minister R. F. ('Pik') Botha and an hour with State President

[32] Ibid., 14.   [33] Ibid.   [34] Ibid.
[35] Diamond, 'Shepherding', 24–5.

P. W. Botha, returned to the United States with 'the true story'. The White minority regime in South Africa is doing a good job, is making many reforms, and deserves our full support, he claimed. He attacked the movement for disinvestment, and instead called for reinvestment in South Africa, urging the good Christian folk of America to buy up krugerrands and to disinvest from companies that join in economic sanctions against South Africa. The number one issue in South Africa is not apartheid, he said, but communism. He said that the only alternative to South Africa's present government is Soviet domination, and that Blacks are better off with what they have now. All the Blacks he talked to in South Africa agreed with him, he insisted; the so-called Black leaders who speak out against the Pretoria government represent only a small vocal segment of the population and are at best misguided and at worst sympathetic to violent communist takeover. Bishop Tutu, for example, is, according to Falwell, a 'phony'.[36]

Pat Robertson's Christian Broadcasting Network (CBN) has led the way in favourable coverage of South Africa: for example, a news feature, 'Who is the ANC?', screened on CBN's '700 Club' on 11 September 1986. The film featured footage shot at close range of two alleged ANC atrocities: one victim was burned alive with a 'necklace'; another was stabbed to death by a crowd of attackers. Interspersed were clips of ANC President Oliver Tambo and Winnie Mandela advocating all-out war against the Pretoria Government. Robertson went on to liken American 'softness' towards the ANC to previous 'betrayals' of Nicaragua's Anastasio Somoza and the Shah of Iran.[37] Robertson is clear that his 'Christian' stance on South Africa is also in line with American interests. In opposing sanctions against South Africa on the grounds that they would put millions of Blacks out of work,

---

[36] *Time* (2 Sept. 1985), 40–3; J. Wallis, 'Falwell's foreign policy', *Sojourners* (Feb. 1986), XV, 5–6. Wallis (ibid., 6) concludes: 'In the name of anti-communism, Jerry Falwell is supporting a regime of thieves and thugs . . . Falwell's foreign policy, like Falwell's gospel, is good news to those who are now in control in places like South Africa, the Philippines, and the United States. But it is decidedly not good news to the poor, as the original gospel message was, and still is. Indeed, it is the poor in South Africa and the Philippines who most welcome the gospel as good news and whose faith is inspiring them to costly commitment and action. In so doing they are becoming a threat to Jerry Falwell's friends in high places. It is the threat of justice that brought Jerry Falwell to South Africa and the Philippines, not the threat of the Soviet Union. When power is most threatened, it desperately seeks religious justification. And there are always those, like Jerry Falwell, who are ready and willing to be the religious apologists for the powers of this world.'

[37] Diamond, 'Shepherding', 24. Diamond goes on to speculate on the source of this footage, since 'it is doubtful that the atrocity scenes . . . could have been filmed by independent newspersons'. She gives evidence for thinking that the footage came from the Reagan Administration.

he added, 'and we do have strategic interests in this country that we must keep in balance with our understandable and appropriate desire to move that nation along'.[38]

This is the standard fare served up by the American religious right. The pressure is relentless. For example, in September 1986, Good News Communications, an Atlanta-based evangelical organization, sent its adherents a newsletter describing a fact-finding tour through South Africa. It contains the whole package: South Africa is a pleasant, peaceful land; true South Africans know that their salvation lies not in the ANC but in Jesus Christ; Soweto contains many millionaires, including Winnie Mandela; Tutu and the ANC have no support among Blacks; Chief Buthelezi, a 'mighty man of God', is the true leader; Blacks overwhelmingly oppose sanctions; apartheid is already being abolished; most South Africans are believing Christians; the ANC is communist — National Executive member Joe Slovo is, in fact, 'a White Lithuanian-Russian who has ruled the ANC and worked for the KGB for many decades'; sanctions will hurt Black Africans ('sanctions are unbiblical'); South Africa is looking after countless Mozambicans fleeing from the socialist violence in Mozambique. Also, significantly, South African minerals are necessary for US survival. The newsletter concludes with a passionate plea to champion the forces of light against the forces of darkness: 'As Christians we should be reaching out to help the people of South Africa, not condemning them to starvation and death . . . Do we stand with the people of the Word against the deadly onslaught of the forces of darkness? Do we stand with Christ against the powers and principalities which oppose him?' It ends with the appeal: 'On September 30 I will be appearing on [Bakker's] PTL programme to discuss Getting the Word Out. Please watch if you can'.[39]

Local South African but US-linked churches further the same message. None more so than the predominantly White Rhema Bible Church, founded in South Africa in 1979 by Ray McCauley, who had trained in Tulsa, Oklahoma, under Kenneth Hagin the founder of Rhema Bible Church.

[38] *Orange County Register* (17 Sept. 1986), A21.
[39] Sent out by Good News Communications, 2876 Mabry Road N.E., Atlanta GA 30319, USA. The points made in this newsletter were painstakingly refuted in an open letter to the authors by Michael Appleby, a Quaker working in Botswana for the Church World Service. Maguire, in dealing with the New Right's racism, asks 'Is it surprising that they have great sympathies for the White Christians of South Africa?'; see Maguire, *The New Subversives*, 106–9. For Falwell's racial attitudes, see Fitzgerald, *Cities on a Hill*, 170–2.

Rhema is best known for its strident preaching of the gospel of prosperity, which certainly has a political role in South Africa, diverting attention from the system which disproportionately favours the Whites, and telling good Christian Whites that faith will bring them even more wealth. But the Church is more overtly political: a newspaper reports that, in South Africa, Rhema's Sunday morning service includes a prayer for the (then) Prime Minister, Cabinet, and 'all those in authority in this land'. The report continues: 'The prayer was followed by a passionate affirmation that "Jesus is Lord over Africa, and no one will take this country away from us. No weapons will prevail against us, this is our land". South African flags flank the desk of Pastor McCauley, and are also in evidence in other parts of his property.'[40]

At Rhema's headquarters there are two flags — significantly, the South African and American. This appals the 'Concerned Evangelicals' of *Evangelical Witness*:

> The most blatant symbol of support for apartheid South Africa and American values is that of the two flags which are hoisted at the Rhema Centre in Randburg, Johannesburg. Blacks who try to go to the Centre have been greeted by the American and South African flags rather than by the flag of the Kingdom of God.
> This shows the degree of insensitivity of evangelical groups and their ignorance about the attitudes of most Blacks in the townships . . . The fact of the matter is that the flag of America symbolizes 'enemy number one' in the minds of most Blacks in the townships, whilst that of South Africa is an insult to their humanity and dignity. It is for this reason that it is absolutely urgent to bring down those flags to replace them with the flag of the Kingdom of God for the sake of the Gospel of the Lord in South Africa.[41]

According to Rhema's Christianity, Jesus is the answer to everything. The *Good News Newsletter* cited above tells the American public that there is a great Christian revival going on in South Africa, and quotes the preacher at Rhema, 'the Black evangelist, Brother Elijah, who forcefully stated that the solution to South Africa's problems was not the communist

[40] *Sunday Tribune* (29 Aug. 1982), quoted in M. de Haas, 'Is millenarianism alive and well in White South Africa?', *Religion in Southern Africa* (1986), VII, 41. For a detailed analysis of Rhema's Christianity, especially its gospel of prosperity, see T. Verryn, *Rich Christian, Poor Christian: An Appraisal of Rhema Teachings* (Pretoria, Ecumenical Research Unit, 1983); The Ecumenical Research Unit, *Throw Yourself Down: A Consideration of the Main Teachings of the Prosperity Cults* (Pretoria, The Unit, n.d.); E. S. Morran and L. Schlemmer, *Faith for the Fearful? An Investigation into New Churches in the Greater Durban Area* (Durban, University of Natal, Centre for Applied Social Sciences, 1984), 5–17.

[41] *Evangelical Witness*, 34.

ANC, but Jesus Christ . . . Only Jesus could change hearts and bring people together'.[42] In Rhema's magazine, Ed Roebert, a South African evangelist, begins an article, 'South Africa stands at the crossroads today. The crossroads are either Christ or communism'. The same article continues with a 'divine prophecy', one 'uttered through' Dave Griffiths of the Hatfield Christian Church, Pretoria:

I am giving to My Kingdom People this nation. Already I have destroyed much that was a hindrance to the fulfilment of My purposes in this land. I have stilled the land. I have brought the land into order. I am causing the people of this nation to look to Me and not to those in the political realm . . .
I have brought to nought the plans of the fathers of anarchy. I have destroyed the sons of anarchy and am releasing My people . . .
I am raising up a Kingdom People to possess this land and you are not to concern yourselves with who will be put in authority. . .
Your land is being fenced in and I want you to know that it is in My plan . . . The coming breakdown of economies in the western nations will not touch you. You will not feel it because I will protect you and I will cause your economy, because it is shut in, to suddenly blossom and I will manifest My Kingdom through it.[43]

God — or at least the God of Ed Roebert and Dave Griffiths — is here plainly on the side of those who declared the State of Emergency: 'I have stilled the land'. God declares himself firmly against the ANC: 'I have brought to nought the plans of the fathers of anarchy'. God tells his people to keep out of politics: 'You are not to concern yourselves with who will be put in authority'. God advocates the gospel of prosperity: 'I will cause your economy . . . to suddenly blossom'. Surprisingly — or perhaps it's not so surprising after all — this God of Rhema, of Hatfield Christian Church, of Ed Roebert and Dave Griffiths, is remarkably similar to the God that P. W. Botha continually invokes.

Ed Roebert, the author of the article just quoted, has told his story, or the story of this Hatfield Baptist Church.[44] This well describes the brand of Christianity for which he stands. Chapter Fourteen is entitled 'To Set the Captives Free', and deals with 'liberation'. The liberation discussed is liberation from alcohol, tobacco, paralysing doctrinal beliefs, law, church tradition, intellectualism, the spirit of criticism, and bad marriages.[45] For

[42] See footnote 39 above.
[43] E. Roebert, 'A spirit-controlled people of destiny', Eagle News (May–July 1987), 6.
[44] J. Michell, Church Ablaze: The Hatfield Baptist Church Story (Basingstoke, Hants, Marshall Pickering, 1985).
[45] Ibid., 149–53.

40

South Africa's millions of other captives — captives of poverty, imprisonment, malnutrition, educational deprivation — not a word. Chapter Eighteen is called 'Radical Christianity'. The 'radical' measures called for are to repent, to be subjects of the Kingdom, to submit to believers' baptism, to abandon spiritual hypocrisy, to come to a personal faith in Christ, to be baptized in the Holy Spirit, to allow the purifying wind of God to blow through oneself.[46] This is the liberation offered; these are the radical measures advocated in South Africa's current economic, political and social circumstances. All is private, personalized, narrowly spiritual; the miracles sought are of tongues and healing; all is intra-ecclesial. There is no threat to any social order here.

Christ for All Nations (CfAN) provides another example. It plays a similar role politically. It has been based in South Africa, although in mid-1986 it moved its headquarters to West Germany. The 'authorized biography' of its founder-director, Reinhard Bonnke, mentions politics only to disclaim any concern with politics at all.[47] But to set a book in contemporary South Africa and to avoid all considerations of inequality, human rights, colour, economic and political discrimination, is hard to do. One could hardly do so unconsciously. It must be the result of a conscious decision to ignore these things. Despite the disclaimer, some deeper attitudes surface. Even to call the Bantustan Venda a 'country'[48] with a 'President'[49] and a 'Head of State'[50] is significant. More significant is Bonnke's sole reaction to the June 1976 Soweto disturbances in which hundreds of Blacks were killed. His team of evangelists had just completed a bicycle crusade through the whole city of Soweto: 'Now Reinhard [Bonnke] knew why God had been in such a hurry and why one hundred bicycles had been needed. Less than that number and they could never have completed the project in time'.[51] CfAN's is a very political role — a role, moreover, very acceptable in some quarters. Bonnke's autobiography makes a good deal of his being received personally by the King of Swaziland,[52] the President of Venda, the Paramount Chief of the Transkei and his Chief of Police.[53] Naturally they would receive him. So,

[46] Ibid.,188–95.
[47] R. Steele, *Plundering Hell: The Reinhard Bonnke Story* (Ravenmoor, South Africa, Sceptre Publications, 1984).
[48] Ibid., 108.   [49] Ibid., 107.   [50] Ibid., 108.
[51] Ibid., 72.   [52] Ibid., 92.   [53] Ibid., 133–4.

undoubtedly, would Pretoria. Pretoria and the Presidents of the Bantustans and their Police Chiefs would prefer to hear (or, better, would prefer that their *subjects* hear) the gospel of Bonnke, Roebert and McCauley rather than the gospel of Tutu, Hurley, Naudé, and Boesak.

This Christianity of Rhema and CfAN and of the revival they represent at best unconsciously acquiesces in the present system, diverting attention from its inherent injustice. At worst, it is deliberately used to perpetuate the privilege of those who benefit from the present system. So South African Christianity now has the same division as Christianity in Latin America. This is even more recent than in Latin America. In South Africa, of course, the use of Christianity for political and economic ends is nothing new. It has been traditional for Pretoria (and for a good proportion of White South Africa) to identify White interests with Christianity; the corresponding identification of Black interests with communism has been just as traditional. In South Africa, then, the words 'Christianity' and 'communism' have ceased to have much meaning. 'Christianity' is used for anything that furthers White interests, 'communism' for anything that threatens them. (South Africa's Suppression of Communism Act effectively defines a communist as anyone who 'aims at bringing about any political, industrial, social or economic change' of which the regime disapproves.)[54] This usage is still found. At the special federal congress of the National Party in Durban in August 1986, with the world listening and expecting him to announce radical reforms, P. W. Botha revealed plainly that, on the contrary, he would preserve intact the basic structure of apartheid. He concluded by invoking Christianity as his justification: 'I look at the constellations in the sky at night and what are the words I see written there? Southern Africa for Christendom!'[55]

However, this outright identification of apartheid with Christianity is perhaps heard less often now, given the broad Christian consensus, transcending denominational, cultural and ethnic divisions, that apartheid is nothing less than a heresy and an obscenity. So the South African regime

[54] South Africa, Suppression of Communism Act (No. 44 of 1950), para. I, sect. 1, subsect. II and III. The Kairos Document treats this well: see *Kairos Document: Challenge to the Church: A Theological Comment on the Political Crisis in South Africa* (Braamfontein, The Kairos Theologians, [1985]), 6; and see also *Evangelical Witness*.
[55] A. Sampson, *Black and Gold: Tycoons, Revolutionaries and Apartheid* (London, Coronet, 1987), 320–1. For examples of the use of theology to support the Afrikaner State, see W. A. de Klerk, *The Puritans in Africa: A Story of Afrikanerdom* (Harmondsworth, Penguin, 1976), esp. 221–2, 252–60.

seems to have changed its approach somewhat. Villa-Vicencio notes that Afrikaner theology has always rested on two apparently conflicting theological approaches: pietism and theological nationalism (or patriotic theology). He has traced a recent shift which has removed the emphasis from the theological nationalism and placed it on the pietism or privatized religion. He traces this shift by analysing the reports of two government commissions, set up only a few years apart.[56] The first was the Steyn Commission (1981), set up to investigate the function of the media in regard to those forces which it perceived to be disruptive of the prevailing order; these forces, according to the Commission, include 'the Soviet, the ANC, terror and other onslaughts and objectives, as well as those liberals and radicals, who from pulpits, platforms or in writing, aim at the subversion of the social order and fabric of our society'.[57] The second was the Eloff Commission (1983), established to investigate those same disruptive forces in regard to the South African Council of Churches (SACC).[58]

Villa-Vicencio notes considerable similarity between the reports, not least the poor scholarship and analysis, the selective use of sources, the non sequiturs and internal contradictions. Both reports oppose any theologically-based dissent from the Pretoria regime. Both attribute the Christian involvement in politics exemplified by the SACC not to the message of the Bible, but to a set of alien influences which prevent the proper understanding of that message. These influences would include liberation theology, Black theology and 'ecumenical' theology.[59] But there is a major difference between the reports. The Steyn Commission would claim to reject all politicized theology on the grounds that religion is being used for political ends. This judgement, though, applied as it is to the social gospel movement, the WCC, the SACC, Black theology, Black consciousness, the theology of liberation, is withheld in the case of the theological nationalism of

[56] C. Villa-Vicencio, 'Theology in the service of the State: The Steyn and Eloff Commissions', in C. Villa-Vicencio and J. W. de Gruchy (eds.), *Resistance and Hope: South African Essays in Honour of Beyers Naudé* (Cape Town, D. Philip, 1985), 112–25. The discussion which follows is taken from Villa-Vicencio's analysis.

[57] South Africa, *Report of the Commission of Inquiry into the Mass Media* [Chairman: M. T. Steyn] (Pretoria, Govt. Printer, RP 89/1981), 1285.

[58] South Africa, *Report of the Commission of Inquiry into the South African Council of Churches* [Chairman: C. F. Eloff] (Pretoria, Govt. Printer, RP 74/1983).

[59] Note, however, how the Steyn Commission approves of 'African theology', supposedly based on a unique and different theological point of view, because it can be used to support special or 'differential' development; see Villa-Vicencio, 'Theology in the service of the State', 117.

Afrikanerdom. Though political theology is rejected in every other case, political theology is valid in the case of Afrikaner civil religion. Easily discernible here is South Africa's traditional patriotic theology, legitimizing and conserving Afrikaner society.

The Eloff Commission, however, chooses another path. Whereas the Steyn Commission saw political theology against the Afrikaner state as a perversion, the Eloff Commission gives no explicit support to *any* political theology. The Eloff Commission turns to a classic secularist response to religion. It maintains that because there are so many conflicting religious views, and no obvious basis for choosing between them, and because there are no definite religious answers to complex political issues, it is far better that religion be restricted to the private sphere, out of the public arena altogether. The Eloff Commission opts for the complete privatization of religion. From this angle it traces the history of the SACC: 'From an organization whose main activity originally was the co-ordination of efforts to spread the Gospel, and whose principal interests lay in spiritual matters, the SACC developed into one largely concerned with political, social and economic issues'.[60] The report moves to curb the social, economic and political involvement of the SACC. It urges that the government control the SACC funds to ensure that they are used for 'only truly spiritual purposes'. The Fund-Raising Act of 1978, which gave exemption to the churches, should be amended. 'To ensure that it cannot be argued that the SACC falls within the exemption, we recommend that the state law advisers prepare a suitable amendment reflecting the idea that only truly spiritual purposes are included. The substitution of the word "spiritual" for "religious" might be adequate.'[61] The submission of the South African Police to the Commission similarly argued that churches should focus their concern on 'personal salvation and conversion'. They claim that the SACC goes beyond its duty: 'It does not involve itself in its primary area, and does not undertake, for instance, large-scale campaigns for money in overseas countries for converting non-Christians in the Republic of South Africa to Christianity'.[62]

Thus there are real differences between the reports. The Steyn Commis-

---

[60] South Africa, *Report of the Commission of Inquiry into the South African Council of Churches*, 427.
[61] Ibid., 443.
[62] Submission to the Eloff Commission: *S. A. Raad van Kerke: 'n Evaluasie deur die S. A. Polisie vir Voorlegging aan die Kommissie van Ondersoek na die SARK*, 10 and 109, cited in Villa-Vicencio, 'Theology in the service of the State', 120.

sion assumes a patriotic, legitimizing function for religion; the Eloff Commission shifts towards a personalized, privatized apolitical form of spirituality. But despite these differences, their *intentions* are the same. The desired effect is the same in both cases. Whether by providing theological justification for the Afrikaner state, or by privatizing Christianity so that it leaves the state unchallenged, the aim is to preserve the status quo, to use Christianity to preserve the privilege of those who have, and to thwart the aspirations of those who have not. Both approaches can be found among government spokesmen, both approaches can be found in the right-wing churches which consciously or unconsciously support the government. But a large sector of South African Christianity has refused to prop up injustice any longer, and has committed itself to work actively for change in the structures of society. Influenced by liberation theology from Latin America, and by Black theology from the United States, a special South African liberation theology has emerged. The SACC and the South African Catholic Bishops Conference — not universally, admittedly, and certainly without carrying all their members with them — and more recently several 'Concerned Evangelicals', have all made their 'option for the poor'.

3 Within Zimbabwe

The use of religion for political purposes is not new to Zimbabwe. In the colonial era, the churches, though with a proud record in the fields of health and education, had little awareness of the role they played in the total structure of colonial society. An insight into the churches' role is provided by the following extract from a letter written by Cecil Rhodes himself to the parents of the Dutch Reformed missionary, Revd A. A. Louw of Morgenster: 'Your son among the natives is worth as much to me as a hundred of my policemen'.[1] Another insight is provided by this Ndau hymn: 'Tora nyika ndipe Jesu, ndodakara ndiye' ('Take all the land, simply give me Jesus and I am happy').[2] The churches doubtless were part of the total colonial structure, but it is anachronistic to be too critical of this: social analysis is a recent discipline, and its association with Marxism meant that Christians were later than most in accepting that way of thinking.

When the liberation struggle began, the picture changed somewhat. Christianity was simply identified with White interests, and communism became identified with the cause of Black nationalism. These identifications were made consciously. Ian Smith proclaimed Rhodesia's independence on 11 November 1965 as a blow struck 'for the preservation of justice, civilization and Christianity', and frequently repeated the idea; Rhodesia's aim, he said, was to preserve 'that Christian civilization which our forefathers brought with them when they pioneered this country and settled here

---

[1] Cited in P. Zachrisson, *An African Area in Change: Belingwe 1894–1946: A Study of Colonialism, Missionary Activity and African Response in Southern Rhodesia* (Gothenburg, Univ. of Gothenburg Press, 1978), 267.

[2] Quoted by T. J. Mafico, 'The Role and Mission of the Church in Independent Zimbabwe', talk at the Zimbabwe Christian Council Symposium on Evangelism, Bulawayo, 13–19 December 1980.

for all time'.[3] D. W. Lardner-Burke, Smith's Minister of Justice, Law and Order, simply identified Rhodesia with Christianity; speaking of the armed struggle in a sermon in the Anglican Cathedral, he claimed 'to be a Christian, therefore I will fight for Christianity'.[4] P. K. van der Byl, Minister of Information, gave a hint of his hidden economic agenda when he declared Rhodesia's ideal to be 'Western Christian free-enterprise Civilization'.[5]

A classic expression of the Christianity versus communism analysis was given by General John Hickman, Commander of the Rhodesian Army, on 30 November 1977:

These so-called Freedom Fighters are fighting to replace a benevolent Christian minority government with a ruthless and totally un-Christian and anti-Christ minority Marxist government. Yet the so-called Christian Western Powers give every aid . . . to those forces of evil . . . . Even more incredible are the actions of the Free World against Christianity here — vilification, sanctions, and abuse. . . . Once a nation has succumbed to Communism — whether by force or infiltration — it remains paralysed in its anti-Christ grip. . . . We have dared to stand against Communism and this is our unforgivable sin. . . . Like the little Dutch boy who stemmed the tide and saved his people, we may yet hold the line and save the world.[6]

By and large, Christians succumbed to this analysis. At one level this is not surprising, given the government's total control of the media. Under constant bombardment from the media, and isolated from developments in the wider world, Rhodesian Christians had little chance to shake off the anti-communist hysteria to which all Western Christians had subscribed at the height of the cold war. There is evidence that the Rhodesian government attempted to capitalize on this situation, and to co-opt the churches in its service. A confidential military 'Directive for National Psychological Campaign' has the heading: 'Target Group: Churches'. Its objective was spelt out clearly: to get Christians 'to recognise the communist terrorist as the national enemy'. It stated that the churches' 'full support should be

[3] *Guardian* (15 Jan. 1975), cited in D. Martin and P. Johnson, *The Struggle for Zimbabwe* (Harare, Zimbabwe Publishing House, 1981), 191. See also M. Lapsley, *Neutrality or Co-option? Anglican Church and State from 1964 until the Independence of Zimbabwe* (Gweru, Mambo Press, 1986), 15–20.
[4] Quoted in I. Linden, *The Catholic Church and the Struggle for Zimbabwe* (London, Longman, 1980), 169.
[5] J. Frederikse, *None but Ourselves: Masses vs. Media in the Making of Zimbabwe* (Harare, Zimbabwe Publishing House,1982), 50; and see also 348.
[6] Ibid., 187.

sought to bring about a quick end to the terrorist war and to promote the benefits of the proposals'.[7]

The Anglican Church, as the most important White church during the colonial years, seemed particularly vulnerable on this score. Among its spokesmen, Bishop Burrough and Dean da Costa seem to have subscribed to this analysis to a large degree, and Fr Arthur Lewis, a senator in Smith's parliament, subscribed totally. He stated, 'We must know what we are defending. This is nothing less than the survival of what is left of Christian civilization and the values and standards, the belief in right and wrong, which communism exists to destroy'.[8] This correlation Lewis was always repeating.[9] Lewis took for granted that Rhodesia was one of Africa's noblest efforts to build a more or less Christian society.[10] He formed the Rhodesia Christian Group, 'to try and stop the flow of Communism at the Zambezi, beyond which it could not spread to destroy western Christian civilization'.[11]

The Catholic Church in general may have succumbed similarly, but some elements were more critical. The Catholic Commission for Justice and Peace mounted considerable opposition to the Smith regime. Its chairman, Bishop Lamont of Umtali, was such a thorn in Smith's side that he was tried, convicted, and deported. The interesting thing is that although Lamont could see through the claim that Christianity equalled White interests, he was as worried about communist influence as Smith. In his 'Open Letter to the Government of Rhodesia', in the *Sunday Mail* of 15 August 1976, he wrote: 'Far from your policies defending Christianity and Western civilization as you claim, they mock the law of Christ and make Communism attractive to the African people'.[12] Lamont could denounce abuses of the Smith government, but he was anything but a liberation theologian in the Latin American sense. Linden claims that it was their inability to adopt the structural thinking of liberation theology that left the Catholic Bishops at sea in their statements about the situation in Rhodesia.[13]

[7] Ibid., 189. The proposals referred to are the British and American proposals which led to the Geneva Conference which began on 28 October 1976.

[8] Ibid., 48.   [9] Ibid., 190–3.

[10] Ibid., 189.   [11] Ibid.

[12] Ibid., 196. For the paradox of Bishop Lamont, see M. Meredith, *The Past Is Another Country: Rhodesia 1890–1979* (London, Deutsch, 1979), 231–7.

[13] Linden, *The Catholic Church*, 240, n.8. R. Riddell, 'The Liberation of Theology: Application to Rhodesia', *The Month* (May 1977), 149–60, compares Segundo's liberation theology with the pastoral letters of the Rhodesian Catholic bishops to show that the bishops were untouched by liberation theology.

Although during the liberation struggle there was little liberation theology within Rhodesia, it was during this time that this way of thinking was developing overseas. During these years the World Council of Churches (WCC) became more influenced by it. This led to the attempt within Rhodesia to discredit it. Lewis's book *Christian Terror* had written on its cover, 'Christ is crucified by those who claim to act for His Church, while His people are murdered in His name'.[14] In conjunction with the Christian League of Southern Africa, the Rhodesian Christian Group published a monthly called *Encounter*. This magazine spent much of its time trying to undermine the influence of the WCC in the region, and the campaign bordered on the hysterical after the WCC in 1978 awarded a grant of US$85 000 to the Patriotic Front of Zimbabwe (for humanitarian purposes) from its special fund to combat racism.[15] Again, it is in keeping with all that we have seen above that in 1979 the disgraced Secretary of the South African Information Department, Eschel Rhoodie, admitted that he had been funding Fr Lewis's group.[16]

So complete was the presentation of the Christianity versus communism picture, that Christians were profoundly alarmed and completely bewildered when Mugabe was elected Prime Minister in 1980, for it was Mugabe in particular who had been painted as the archetypal Marxist thug. Mugabe acknowledged this in addressing the heads of religious denominations in 1982:

I personally was portrayed as a communist man-eater, my party as an inhuman, terrorist organization bent on the destruction of society and the basic values it cherished. The communist bogey was the most common weapon that they effectively employed to frighten you all and get you scared of Mugabe and his ZANU(PF) and ZANLA. Alas, many, if not most, of you buckled before this propaganda, gulped down many doses of it, and thus became its believers. We are aware, however, that some of you refused to swallow it and saw in our actions a motivation deriving from justice.[17]

It is really since Independence that the division within Zimbabwean Christianity has become unmistakable, the division between the two types of Christianity discussed above. The one, like the liberation theology of Latin America, tries to incorporate some structural awareness; the most

---

[14] Frederikse, *None but Ourselves*, 192.
[15] Ibid., 193.   [16] Ibid., 189–90.
[17] Address to Heads of Denominations, 30 April 1982, Press Release, Dept. of Information, P. O. Box 8150, Causeway, Harare.

prominent advocate of such an approach has been the Revd Canaan Banana, President of Zimbabwe from 1980 to 1987. The other lies clearly in the stream of Christianity stemming from the southern United States, and churches of this stamp have mushroomed in Zimbabwe since about 1982. It is to a discussion of some individual churches or ministries embodying this second type of Christianity that we now turn.

Campus Crusade

Behind Campus Crusade stands Henrietta Mears, a wealthy Californian dispensationalist who in 1949 was instrumental in launching Billy Graham. Part of the cold-war evangelical revival, she sought an answer to what she considered the growing menace of communism. She regarded college campuses as the key to world leadership and world revival, and though motivated by her dread of communism, she self-consciously took over communist methods of organization; for example, in her refinement of the cell system, two friends pray and work to convert a third, and then this third forms another cell to do likewise, and so on. A protégé of hers, a Californian Presbyterian called Bill Bright, founded Campus Crusade in 1951 on the campus of the University of California at Los Angeles, and he developed her techniques.[18]

Thus, as one would expect, Campus Crusade is rabidly anti-communist. Bright begins his *Revolution Now* with a catalogue of the world's ills, and then states: 'Underneath all these frightening characteristics of our day, the diabolical manipulations of international communism are bringing us ever closer to universal tyranny. According to present schedules, and apart from a spiritual revolution through divine intervention, communist conquest of the world is assured in this generation'.[19] Hence the need for Campus Crusade; to galvanize 'Christians' into staging their own revolution, to win the whole world 'for Christ',[20] by beating the communists at their own game. Bright and Campus Crusade are totally dispensationalist. Their job is to fulfil the 'great commission' of Matthew 28: 19 because they believe that this will be the last generation before the second coming of

[18] B. Bright, *Revolution now* (San Bernardino CA, Campus Crusade, 1969), 193–207; Kickham, 'The theology of nuclear war', 12–13.

[19] Bright, *Revolution now*, 11–12.

[20] Ibid., 185–9.

Christ: 'I am absolutely convinced that the Great Commission will be fulfilled in our generation'.[21]

Campus Crusade attempts to do this through a variety of ministries. It is active on over 700 university and college campuses in the United States. Campus Crusade targeted the campus of the University of Los Angeles at Berkeley for saturation evangelism in 1967 in an effort to break the movement there against the Vietnam War. They went on to hold 'alternate' rallies in competition with the anti-war protests at other campuses. (It was during those years, when Reagan was Governor of California, that Bright met Reagan and they became firm friends.) Campus Crusade not only focuses on universities: it has a policy of targeting leaders. It is very strong in Washington and at the United Nations through its 'Christian Embassies'.[22] It also has a world-wide mission, and is particularly involved in Central America, Africa, South-East Asia, in the front lines of United States global interest. In 1985, Campus Crusade began experimenting with satellite video conferences. The event Explo '85 linked up audiences in fifty-four countries. Main speakers included Billy Graham and the Argentinian evangelist Luis Palau whom I have mentioned above. During the four-day event, Bright himself gave keynote addresses in (significantly?) South Korea, the Philippines, West Berlin, and Mexico City. Bright dreams of five million, then fifty million, disciplined recruits working under his direction to bring in the last harvest.

Bright's Christianity is a classic illustration of the current American evangelical revival. First, everything is personal and privatized. When Bright speaks of social involvement, especially through his 'Agape Movement', a Christian service corps modelled on the Peace Corps, it is all in terms of an individual's influencing others for good; there is no attempt to address the systems in which individuals live.[23] Secondly, although the whole message is billed as 'Christian' and non-political, this is manifestly not the case. His approving official biographer can write: 'Insiders know that Bill can be very naïve politically. One of his closest associates had to

---

[21] Ibid., 187. Hal Lindsey, whose dispensationalist 'farrago of nonsense' we met above, started out working for Campus Crusade at the University of California at Berkeley; see Jones, 'Reagan's religion', 62.

[22] See Jones, 'Reagan's religion', 65.

[23] See R. Quebedeaux, *I Found It: The Story of Bill Bright and Campus Crusade* (London, Hodder, 1980), 171–4, 119–22, 149, 157–60. This entirely private and personal Christianity is evident in the Campus Crusade Manual, *Ten Basic Steps towards Christian Maturity* (San Bernardino CA, Campus Crusade, 1965).

demonstrate to him, on a blackboard, that his "non-political" stance really was political; it didn't appear neutral at all, but rang conservative. Bill was amazed.'[24]

In the mid-1970s, Campus Crusade's clear involvement in politics was established. A clear inter-relationship was established between the people involved in Bright's Christian Embassy, the Campus Crusade board of directors, the Freedom Foundation, and Third Century Publishers, founded in 1974 to publish books and other materials to articulate an ideologically conservative political and economic philosophy allegedly based on biblical principles. His biographer absolves Bright himself, but does not deny what was going on: 'It is manifestly clear that a conspiracy of some sort was being planned by people associated with the aforementioned [Bright] organisations and with Bill himself'.[25]

His biographer admits that Bright is a classic example of a 'bi-modal' thinker; he sees dualism in every facet of life.[26] If the evil of communism is basic for him, equally basic is the identification of America with Christianity. This gives Campus Crusade a predictable role outside the United States. In Latin America, Campus Crusade sees itself as the shock troops in countering liberation theology. Liberation theology Christians are considered nothing more than 'masked communists'. Materials published and distributed by Campus Crusade have fostered the United States' Latin American policy, identified the American system as an expression of Christian ideas, and have claimed that the formation of the United States is the 'single most important event since the birth of Christ'.[27]

Campus Crusade in South Africa, as in Latin America, is not primarily a campus ministry. In 1983 it split into two 'sister' organizations, one White and Afrikaans-speaking, one Black; both are under the same board of directors. The poorer Black 'sister' employs about ten Black couples who work at community evangelism in Black townships and in the 'homelands'. About 80 per cent of the total resources go to the White 'sister' which has 120 full-time staff, 32 'associate staff' who volunteer for eight to ten hours a week, 17 salaried secretarial staff, and an annual budget of over two

[24] Quebedeaux, *I Found It*, 190.
[25] Ibid., 188–9; see also 186–91. For the whole affair, see J. Wallis and W. Michaelson, 'The plan to save America', *Sojourners* (Apr. 1976), 3–12.
[26] Quebedeaux, *I Found It*, 186–7.
[27] See Huntington, 'God's saving plan', 31. Huntington's article is a mine of information on Campus Crusade's operations in Central America.

million rand. This group has successfully evangelized Afrikaner business executives, government bureaucrats, academics and others of the White élite. They hold 'executive seminars' and marriage workshops for business-men and their wives at expensive resort hotels. The organization attempts to appear apolitical and neutral, but it has distributed secretly a speech by right-wing activist Ed Cain, attacking Christian opponents of the apartheid system. 'Campus Crusade is a perfect example of an American evangelical group that has completely adjusted and assimilated to the apartheid sys-tem'.[28]

In Zimbabwe, Campus Crusade has functioned since 1979 as Life Ministries.[29] Besides five administrative staff, it has ten full-time ministerial staff, of whom six are expatriates from the United States. Most of the Americans have been trained at the Campus Crusade international head-quarters in California. Campus Crusade's ministries in Zimbabwe are divided into three sections, and are similar to those in other countries. First, Campus Crusade provides a chaplaincy at the University of Zimbabwe, focusing mainly on those not served by existing chaplains. Secondly, it has ministries which it labels 'church resources'. These include training pastors or lay-people in local churches; screening Campus Crusade's 'Jesus' Film (in Shona, Ndebele, Tonga and English); and relief work such as the distri-bution of clothes and maize meal. This relief distribution it accomplishes through local churches, for example, the Assembly of God Church in Hwange, the Evangelical Alliance Mission (TEAM) at Mukumbura, and the Church of the Nazarene in Bulawayo. Thirdly, it has a ministry which it calls 'executive ministry', which comprises seminars and retreats for govern-ment or business people which are held at Kariba, Fothergill Island, or Nyanga, and which offer senior executives a chance to 'refocus their priorities'. As well as these ordinary ministries, they organized the link-up for Explo '85 at the Harare International Conference Centre, and fifty-nine local churches participated in this. Campus Crusade's funding is both local and foreign, the foreign funding coming mainly from the United States. Campus Crusade is in other countries of the area, too, and their South Central Region is effectively all the independent states of Southern Africa. The regional office is in Swaziland, with Nairobi the headquarters for the continent.

[28] L. Jones, 'Right-wing evangelicals and South Africa', *Moto* (Apr. 1988), 12.
[29] Interview with directors, Harare, 15 July 1987.

53

Youth With A Mission (YWAM)

YWAM (pronounced 'wy-wam') was founded in 1960 by Loren Cunningham, as an inter-denominational youth missionary movement. By 1970, the first YWAM training centre was established in Lausanne, Switzerland, and over 100 exist now in 60 countries as spring-boards for mission. By 1985, it had 5 100 long-term missionaries, 190 permanent YWAM bases. In 1985 it sent out 15 000 short-term missionaries, more, it claims, than any other mission. Since its inception, over 100 000 YWAMers have gone to more than 200 countries of the world. Its book listing 'Global Opportunities in Youth with a Mission' gives its 190 YWAM addresses from American Samoa to Zimbabwe, with contact names, but includes the caveat on every other page not to mention YWAM in the address.[30]

These missionaries take part in three kinds of ministry: evangelism, training and relief work. Their evangelism, based on the great commission of Matthew 28: 19, aims to reach every people on the globe. Training involves schools for missionary service. Relief work extends to working with refugees — on four continents — and in hospitals and on food programmes. No one in YWAM receives a salary. Some receive support from their home church or family, but ministry operating costs are usually covered by the support of local churches or by local donations. YWAM's headquarters are on Hawaii, where in 1980 it began its Pacific and Asia Christian University (PACU).

Cunningham is a pentecostal, with a strong belief in miracles. He, too, is a 'bi-modal' thinker: 'In reality there are only two kingdoms: light and darkness. Spiritual, intellectual and physical reality are all blended together within these two kingdoms. They are there at all times'.[31] His politicized Christianity is clear from the following: Latin America is

the place of revolutionary struggle in the '80s — a period designated by the Kremlin to be the decade to take over the youth of Latin America . . . A place [of struggle] between the super powers and between the *super* super powers, God and Satan. Satan is trying to polarize the spiritual options in Latin America by trying to convince the people that they have two choices — the choice of liberation theology or the

---

[30] O'Brien, 'The Christian underground', 34–5. Figures are taken from YWAM's magazine, *World Christian* (Jan. 1986), 19–21. See also L. Cunningham, 'Taking the Gospel into all the world with signs following', *People of Destiny* (July–Aug. 1985), 25–9 [published from 3515 Randolph Rd, Wheaton MD 20902, USA].

[31] Cunningham, 'Taking the Gospel into all the world', 26.

choice of dictatorship . . . God has a third alternative and that is revival and reformation.[32]

Here we see the '*super* super powers' allied with their champions, Russia and America, and the discrediting of liberation theology. America is an instrument in God's hands. Cunningham continues:

The United States is in a place to go on with their [*sic*] God-called role of world leadership for world evangelism . . . If we accept that leadership we will go on to the *greatness that God intended for our nation in other ways*, but that is the key . . .'[33]

Cunningham spent 1960–1963 in West Africa, and analyses the African situation thus:

When you say Africa I see a picture of the Sahara advancing at six miles a year. I see death going before it, and symbolic of that death the advance of the Moslem religion . . . The religion and the desert speak of one another. They are death. Africa is a continent in conflict, with its many spiritual forces on a collision course. On the one hand you have the animistic tribal religions of witchcraft but on the other Christianity . . . Of course, there is the introduction of the Cubans and Soviets and the Chinese in Angola and Mozambique, but the big overriding battle is a continent on a spiritual collision course.[34]

YWAM's literature cites support from Campus Crusade's Bill Bright, from Pat Robertson, and from Tim LaHaye. At the 25th anniversary celebration in 1985 a letter from Reagan praised YWAM for 'a justly renowned reputation for upholding the principles of morality and the spiritual values which have traditionally guided our nation'.[35]

YWAM began in Rhodesia in the 1970s, but closed in 1977 from lack of personnel because of the war.[36] It was reconstituted in 1981 by a couple who had previously run their own personal ministry in Bulawayo. In 1987, YWAM had seven full-time workers in Harare (five White Zimbabweans, one South African, one North American) and six in Bulawayo (five Black Zimbabweans and one North American). The director in Harare was also responsible for two in Lusaka and four in Mozambique. YWAM's work in Zimbabwe is in the three areas characteristic of YWAM everywhere. Its evangelization is directed to helping local, particularly indigenous, churches, or to planting churches where none existed before. Its training

---

[32] Ibid., 28. [33] Ibid., emphasis added. [34] Ibid.
[35] O'Brien, 'The Christian underground', 34.
[36] Interview with director, Harare, 7 Aug. 1987.

takes many forms: it has its own in-house Discipleship Training School twenty-three kilometres from Bulawayo; it runs discipleship training in youth groups for periods of five-to-six months, and leadership training for indigenous churches particularly. Its relief work bears mainly on food relief along the Mozambique border, and medical assistance in Mozambique —
a YWAM American volunteer nurse was one of the six missionaries abducted from central Mozambique by the MNR from May until August 1987. The numbers on short-term mission work can vary. At one time a group of forty on their way to a YWAM convention in Durban stopped over in Zimbabwe for three weeks' concentrated evangelization. Other teams conducted a similar short blitz among farmers in the Karoi area. At another time four British students spent a holiday on evangelization in Mutare. The advantage of such short-term work is that it can be done on a tourist visa.

Full Gospel Businessmen's Fellowship International (FGBMFI)

The FGBMFI began in 1952 when a small group of businessmen met for breakfast in Los Angeles. It was organized and initially funded by Demos Shakarian, a prominent Californian dairyman, whose father had emigrated from Armenia in 1905. Shakarian was led by a vision of world-wide revival which he thought would herald the imminent return of Christ. Since then, FGBMFI has organized 600 000 men into local chapters in 92 countries.

It is non-denominational, including Catholic and main-line Protestant charismatics, but it is predominantly pentecostal, characterized by faith-healing and praying in tongues and prophecy. The doctrinal statement to which all adherents subscribe states:

We believe that the Bible in its entirety is the inspired word of God and infallible rule of faith and conduct ... We believe in Divine healing, through faith ... in the baptism of the Holy Spirit accompanied by the initial physical sign of speaking with other tongues ... We believe in ... the imminent personal return of the Lord Jesus Christ. We believe in intensive world evangelism and missionary work in accordance with the Great Commission, with signs following.

Thus adherents believe that they are living in the last days and are helping to organize the last harvest heralding the second coming. They hold local breakfasts and dinners, regional and world conventions, and publish books, pamphlets and the magazine *Voice*.

President Reagan has close ties with it. It was an FGBMFI member who on 20 September 1970 prophesied that Reagan would be President if he 'continued to walk in God's way'. Reagan credited an FGBMFI prayer group with instantly healing his ulcers during his term as Governor of California.[37] His administration includes a number of members. The best known is James G. Watt, Secretary of the Interior from 1981 to 1983. Watt's address, 'Battle for America', delivered at the 30th World Convention of the FGBMFI in Detroit, 5–9 July 1983, is a good example of civil religion, glorifying the United States. Extolling political and spiritual freedom, as he understands them, he continued: 'In the destiny that God has provided, there is one moment in time where these two political streams — political liberty and spiritual freedom — have been allowed to come together and form the mighty river called America — our America'. His final sentence calls for commitment both to Christ and to America. After citing the American national anthem, he says: 'How appropriate that we who have committed our lives to Christ also rededicate ourselves to America — to liberty and to freedom, so that this nation will endure for generations to come'.[38]

Besides government officials and businessmen, the FGBMFI includes many in the military, many in the nuclear chain of command, and some, like Sanford McDonnell, chairman of the board of McDonnell Douglas, who control the high-tech military industries that build the United States' nuclear arsenal.[39]

The Fellowship has chapters throughout the world. It is particularly active in those parts of the world where the United States has strong interests, or where the United States is fearful of civil disturbance or Soviet influence. Rios Montt, the former dictator of Guatemala (June 1982 – August 1983) spoke at the world convention in 1984, and at one time it was claimed that the Presidents of Guatemala, El Salvador and Honduras were all members. An article in *Voice* claims that, 'We are convinced that when we reach top leaders in business and government, the difference Christ makes in them is felt through the nation. In our meetings with these men we do not offer political or financial solutions. We present Jesus Christ as the only answer for their national and personal needs'. It goes on to quote the conclusion to

[37] *Los Angeles Times* (15 July 1978); see Jones, 'Reagan's religion', 62.
[38] *Voice* (Nov. 1983), XXXI, 3–4, 28.
[39] An interview with McDonnell is printed in *Voice* (Aug. 1986), XXXIV, 3–9. For FGBMFI's links with the military–nuclear–industrial complex, see Kickham, 'The theology of nuclear war', 16–17. The prominence of such believers in the US military–industrial complex, few of whom have any horror of nuclear war, many of whom believe they will be 'raptured' before it breaks out, and who believe that nuclear war is decreed by God Himself, is a phenomenon that needs to be widely publicized.

a speech delivered by General Policarpo Paz Garcia, President (until January 1982) of Honduras, at an FGBMFI banquet held in his honour: 'Now I would like to conclude this evening by placing my trust in the Lord Jesus Christ. I know that by trusting Jesus, He will bless our land of Honduras. Jesus Christ is Lord!'[40] But such lofty sentiments cannot disguise the fact that Honduras is little more than an 'American military laboratory', and power and authority belong to the American ambassador, the commander of the army, and the President, in that order of importance.[41]

The FGBMFI regularly organizes 'airlifts', by which members fly at their own expense to target countries where they organize breakfasts and banquets and spread their version of the gospel to national élites. In January 1986 an airlift went to the Philippines; 1986 also saw airlifts to El Salvador, Guatemala, Costa Rica, Mexico and South Africa.

The autobiography of founder Demos Shakarian well illustrates this brand of Christianity.[42] First, it is strongly pentecostal: spectacular miracles abound, including miracles over nature and raising from the dead.[43] It well illustrates another pentecostal characteristic, too: although Shakarian would claim that the Bible 'in its entirety is the inspired Word of God and infallible rule of faith and conduct', there are, at most, five biblical references in the entire book — Leviticus 22: 20, Deuteronomy 28 and 1 Corinthians 12 are the only obvious ones. What is all important is not the Bible but personal inspiration and illumination. Secondly, the gospel of prosperity is pervasive: it is his fidelity to God that has made Shakarian the biggest dairyman in the world.[44] God tells him which cows to buy; God told another how to design the plough which made his fortune.[45] Thirdly, and most importantly for our purposes, the book is characterized by a complete ignorance of the social role of religion. It is noteworthy that the only airlift he describes is one to Haiti. Papa Doc Duvalier, among the most distasteful dictators of recent times, invited the Fellowship, who held a mass revival crusade, complete with Duvalier senators and generals on the platform. Shakarian

---

[40] N. Peyton, 'Ambassador to a world in conflict', reprinted in *African Voice* (1982), iii, 16–19.

[41] E. R. F. Sheehan, 'The Country of Nada', *New York Review of Books* (27 Mar. 1986), 17.

[42] D. Shakarian as told to J. and E. Sherrill, *The Happiest People on Earth: The Long-awaited Personal Story of Demos Shakarian* (Old Tappan NJ, Spire Books, 1975).

[43] Hollenweger notes that even pentecostals are sceptical of accounts of raisings from the dead, *The Pentecostals*, 360.

[44] Shakarian, *The Happiest People on Earth*, 75.

[45] Ibid., 140–1.

describes how thousands were won to Jesus, how voodoo priests were routed, and disarmingly notes that, among all this, political questions 'just never came up'.[46] Shakarian expresses some surprise that a grateful Duvalier found time to give the businessmen an audience at the end of the crusade. But there is nothing surprising in that; even if the businessmen did not, Duvalier understood the support such religion offers to regimes like his own. It was precisely to counter the rise of liberation theology that Duvalier began inviting these evangelicals to Haiti in the 1960s. As the regime became more and more oppressive — leading eventually to the overthrow of the Duvaliers, though not, alas, of Duvalierism — the influx increased, so that, by 1987, of the six thousand Americans in the country, four to five thousand were evangelicals: a ratio of almost one missionary for every thousand Haitians. This makes the Western world's poorest country — and there can be few run more unjustly — per capita 'probably the most evangelicized country in the world'.[47]

In Zimbabwe, the FGBMFI began with eleven members in 1983.[48] It was founded by a South African group who travelled to the country to begin it. The Zimbabwe Chapter was under the control of the South African Chapter until 1985. There are now Chapters in Harare, Bulawayo, Karoi, Gweru. In Harare, the group meets monthly, alternating a lunch one month, and a dinner the next. About thirty attend the lunches, about sixty the dinners. Altogether, about sixty belong, of whom about five per cent are Black. Members are drawn from a variety of professions and lines of business. Most come from pentecostal churches like the Living World Tabernacle, Mabelreign Chapel, Faith Ministries, Rhema, Northside Community Church and the King's Church. Members bring other professional and business people to the functions, endeavouring to get them to make a commitment to Christ. It is not a fund-raising organization, although the annual subscription is Z$25 which enables it to make donations to various ministries, especially those of pastors who belong to the group or who come to address them. The Harare secretary said simply, 'We don't interest ourselves in politics . . . I personally am too concerned with studying the Bible'.

[46] Ibid., 177.
[47] See M. Massing, 'Haiti: The new violence', *New York Review of Books* (3 Dec. 1987), 50–1.
[48] Interview with secretary, Harare, 3 Nov. 1987.

Jimmy Swaggart Ministries

The Jimmy Swaggart World Ministry Centre in Baton Rouge, Louisiana, is a complex of concrete-columned white buildings spread over 257 acres. It includes the Jimmy Swaggart Bible College with 1 400 students. Its Vance Teleproduction Centre prepares the most widely-viewed religious television programmes in the world. Edited versions of crusades and Bible classes are screened by 200 stations in the United States, and are screened in 145 countries in English and fifteen foreign languages. The world-wide audience was estimated in 1987 at 500 million. These viewers in 1987 contributed US$135 million of the revenue of US$150 million, at a rate of over US$500 000 every working day. The remainder came from the sales of gospel records, tapes, Bibles, books and T-shirts through one of the biggest mail-order businesses in the United States. Fund-raising letters are mailed at the rate of seven million pieces a day, from a mail-room with its own ZIP code. Swaggart lives at the Centre in a US$1,5 million home set in twenty landscaped acres. His son has a similar home nearby. Swaggart flies a private Gulfstream jet once owned by the Rockefeller family. The executive board of Jimmy Swaggart Ministries is effectively controlled by family members; in all, twenty-two Swaggart relatives are on the pay-roll. At the Centre, a computerized printing plant prepares over 24 million copies of pamphlets with titles such as *A Letter to My Catholic Friends*, *When God Fights Russia*, *Music, the New Pornography?*, as well as album covers. Jimmy Swaggart claims to be the biggest-selling gospel artist of all time, with over thirteen million units sold. Music seems to be in the blood. Jimmy Swaggart was brought up with his double first cousin, Jerry Lee Lewis, who (along with Elvis Presley, Chuck Berry, and Little Richard) was to become one of the four pillars of rock 'n' roll. The two had a rather wild childhood in the small-town Southern back-water of Ferriday, 80 miles up the Mississippi from Baton Rouge. His whole extended family was part of the Southern Bible Belt, and he himself as a thirteen-year old had a religious experience during which he actually 'saw the Beast'.

If Pat Robertson appears the most sophisticated and urbane of the television preachers, Jimmy Swaggart must be near the other end of the spectrum. According to Steve Chapple — in a racy article which, nevertheless, captures well the ethos of America's Deep South — all the major televangelists when compared with Swaggart seem like 'slimy unctuous poseurs . . . so patently false they would cause a stuffed dog to bark out'.[49] Jimmy Swaggart is different from the others: 'Jimmy Lee Swaggart *lives* movies like *Poltergeist* and *The Exorcist*. Jimmy Lee has beaten back the Devil/Bear/Beast in the middle of the night. Jimmy Lee Swaggart understands the hairy swamp monkey of fear and desire that is the American subconscious, because Jimmy Lee feels *the fire*.' Though the intellectuals and media people of California and the eastern seaboard might be at a total loss when confronted with Swaggart, 'it's Jimmy Lee that the American people, God help us, really seem to juice for'.[50]

The Swaggart phenomenon cannot be understood apart from his roots in Ferriday, Louisiana — in Chapple's words, 'easily the ugliest place that I have ever driven a rent-a-car through'.[51] Here, the Ku Klux Klan firebombed houses during the civil-rights period. Here live

God-fearing folk, good Americans who know that it is only a fundamentalist deity that protects them from the terrors of modern life should the devil of progress and disruption break asunder their family, put the women to work, annihilate the developing fetus, hook the children on dope and New York ideas, threaten to slay them with silver clouds of radiation.[52]

Swaggart's is a swamp religion, his deity a swamp God. He takes the fight to the devil, whom he familiarly addresses as 'Old Splitfoot'. He is fiercely anti-communist, and almost as fiercely anti-Catholic: 'Most Catholics are Catholics two times a year; once at Mardi Gras and once at . . . I can't think of the other'.[53] He has attacked Catholicism for 'damning the deceived souls of multitudinous millions'.[54] He believes the Bible is literally true in every respect, and politics can be read off from the Bible.[55]

Though Ferriday's current mayor says Swaggart was never a racist, Swaggart has definite ideas about modern Africa; what happened during the

[49] S. Chapple, 'Whole lotta savin' goin' on: The gospel according to Jimmy Lee Swaggart', *Mother Jones* (July–Aug. 1986), 42. The details of Swaggart's Ministries are taken from Chapple's article and from the *Los Angeles Times* (14 Mar. 1988), Part I, 1, 16–17.

[50] Chapple, 'Whole lotta savin' goin' on', 42, emphasis in original.

[51] Ibid., 86.

[52] Ibid.

[53] Ibid., 41–2. For a discussion of Swaggart's 'theology', including his booklet on Catholicism, see P. Gifford, ' "Africa shall be saved": An appraisal of Reinhard Bonnke's pan-African crusade', *Journal of Religion in Africa* (1987), XVII, 79–80.

[54] *Time* (7 Mar. 1988), 51.

[55] Chapple, 'Whole lotta savin' goin' on', 44.

colonial period is far better than what is taking place now: 'If most Africans had their way and if they knew a little bit about colonialism, and they could vote without fear of reprisal . . . they would vote 90% to go back under what they were under' — that is, under colonialism with White rulers. He has 'been all over Africa and South Africa'.[56] He has called South Africa a 'godly' country, and has hosted representatives of the racially segregated 'coloured' parliament on TV. He has told viewers that the struggle in South Africa has nothing to do with race, but is instead a battle between Christ and Antichrist — the White regime representing Christ and 'Christian civilization'.[57]

Evangelical Witness attacks Swaggart bitterly and by name:

We as 'Concerned Evangelicals' have been outraged by the blatant way in which American evangelists like Jimmy Swaggart come here to South Africa in the midst of our pain and suffering, even unto death, and pronounce that 'apartheid is dead', simply because he addressed a multiracial gathering at Ellis Park Rugby stadium, or maybe for the more serious reason of the need to support South Africa because it profits the West at our expense.

It goes on 'to prove how Jimmy Swaggart really served the interests of this brutal apartheid system' by noting that after the declaration of the State of Emergency on 12 June 1986 SATV replayed his sermon:

In his sermon he called on South Africans to promote and defend what he called Western civilization, Western freedoms, and democracy. Many Black South Africans were outraged by the sermon and the arrogance of a foreigner who comes to tell us that apartheid is dead when we know that it is alive and well, and that it kills.[58]

He does his bit for Latin America, too: in Argentina (where he dined with the sister of the President), he boasts that 500 000 Catholics have 'come to Christ' in the space of two years.[59] Thus has developed a world-wide ministry for someone who is virtually incomprehensible outside America's Deep South.

On 21 February 1988 the future of Swaggart's ministry was put in some doubt when he confessed before a congregation of 7 500 at his Family Worship Centre to 'specific incidents of moral failure'. The incidents were

[56] Ibid., 45.
[57] Jones, 'Right-wing evangelicals and South Africa', 12.
[58] *Evangelical Witness*, 31–2.
[59] Chapple, 'Whole'lotta savin' goin' on', 41.

not specified but they involved prostitutes of the less-reputable parts of New Orleans. The Louisiana District Presbytery of the Assemblies of God suspended him from the pulpit for three months, but the national 240-member General Presbytery increased the suspension to one year. Swaggart refused to observe the longer suspension, and was consequently defrocked by the General Presbytery on 8 April. Swaggart then declared his ministry independent and resumed his ministry on 22 May. This 'moral failure' has undoubtedly affected his ministry. In the first half of 1988 the organization was forced to lay off a hundred staff members and halt construction projects, at least three of the Ministry's twelve board members resigned, several members of the Bible College faculty departed for posts elsewhere, three cable television networks (CBN, the PTL Inspiration Cable Network, and BET) cancelled Swaggart's TV programmes, and contributions dropped from US$500 000 a day to less than the US$350 000 that Swaggart says is needed daily to keep his world-wide operations solvent.[60]

Jimmy Swaggart Ministries have been operating in Zimbabwe since January 1985.[61] In Zimbabwe there is no strictly evangelistic mission, merely an office for Jimmy Swaggart's Relief Ministries and Jimmy Swaggart Child Care International, which are for aid rather than for proselytizing. The Zimbabwe operation has a staff of four in Harare, and another four in Chipinge near the Mozambique border. Their budget for 1986 was Z$2 500 000. A fraction of this goes in small grants, for medicine to the Evangelical Alliance Mission (TEAM), for a mobile unit at Chipinge, for churches in drought-stricken areas, but the bulk of it goes to Mozambican refugees in Tongogara refugee camp at Chipinge, and Nyangombe at Nyanga, and to Mozambique itself. Money comes every month from the United States; it is changed into local currency here, where the supplies are bought, and then they are trucked to the recipients. All this relief work, the director asserts, is done in co-operation with the Zimbabwe government ministry responsible for social welfare. The supplies for Mozambique are trucked through to Beira where they are handed to Mozambican officials and put in a bonded warehouse until released to the Mozambican distribution

[60] *Guardian* (22 Feb. 1988), 1; ibid. (23 Feb. 1988), 2; *Newsweek* (29 Feb. 1988), 20–1; *Time* (7 Mar. 1988), 50–3; ibid. (11 Apr. 1988), 58; *Newsweek* (7 Mar. 1988), 43; *Los Angeles Times* (26 Mar. 1988), Part II, 6–7; ibid. (30 Mar. 1988), Part I, 12; ibid. (31 Mar. 1988), Part I, 1, 28–9; ibid. (23 May 1988), 1, 3; *San Francisco Chronicle* (22 Feb. 1988), 1; ibid. (23 Feb. 1988), A3; *The Observer* (28 Feb. 1988), 11; *Orange County Register* (20 May 1988), A15.
[61] Interview with director, Harare, 6 Aug. 1987.

committee. At the Mozambican end, Jimmy Swaggart Ministries work with local churches — in Beira, the Baptist and Pentecostal Churches, and the Church of the Nazarene.

This concern with government approval and bonded warehouses is important, because of suspicion surrounding Jimmy Swaggart Ministries that they are supporting the Renamo rebels. The suspicion has arisen, not simply because of Swaggart's strident anti-communism and the religious right's humanitarian aid to the Contras in Nicaragua. Nor does it arise merely because Swaggart literature was discovered in 1985 at a captured Renamo base.[62] It has arisen because in 1986 in Washington a spokesman for the pro-Renamo 'Mozambique Information Office' stated that Jimmy Swaggart was providing aid through Assembly of God Churches in Renamo-held territory. When asked, Swaggart's aides would not comment on this claim.[63] The Zimbabwean officials of Jimmy Swaggart Ministries are well aware of the suspicion, and thus claim to go to any lengths to show how groundless it is. The White Zimbabwean director in Harare was prepared to show me all official record books, with Zimbabwean and Mozambican official stamps proving that the two governments can account for every unit of aid in question. He also claimed to understand the government's suspicion, but insisted that it is groundless.

World Vision International (WVI)

Historically, World Vision has been profoundly distrusted by other aid agencies, the main complaints being: its linking of aid to proselytizing, even using aid to pressurize recipients to accept evangelical Christianity; its high administration costs; its refusal to face the root causes of the suffering it tries to alleviate; its insistence that it should never 'take sides' politically, but remain 'neutral' in every situation; and the disputed claims in its appeals concerning alleged partnership with other churches and organizations.[64]

World Vision is bedevilled by its history. It grew out of evangelical Christianity during the cold war when conservative evangelicalism was closely identified with American anti-communism. (Thus it cannot strictly

---

[62] S. Askin, 'Mozambique terrorists backed by evangelical right', *National Catholic Reporter* (18 Sept. 1987), 6.

[63] J. Friedland in an Inter-Press Service Feature dated Washington, 28 Oct. 1986. See discussion in S. Askin, 'Is religious freedom misused in Zimbabwe?', *Moto* (Oct. 1987), 9–10.

[64] For a full discussion of these and the following points, see S. Askin, 'Hostility, conflict engulf World Vision', *National Catholic Reporter* (23 Apr. 1982), 9–11, 35–6.

be called part of the New Right: it emerged at the same time as Billy Graham.) It was founded by Robert Pierce who had started out making 'mission films' in China and Korea. The anti-communism was still strong when World Vision began operations in Vietnam. Its seemingly limitless funds and large headquarters opposite the United States embassy emphasized its close links with the United States Agency for International Development (USAID). Its willingness to report its activities to USAID led to charges of informing the CIA. At the same time it continually refused to join with other Vietnam aid agencies in protesting against human-rights violations or the maltreatment of refugees. This was the time when aid agencies were becoming polarized politically, and World Vision (along with organizations such as Catholic Relief Services) was seen as definitely on the right, and others, such as the American Friends Service Committee and the Mennonite Central Committee, as on the left.

Friction among relief agencies turned into a raging battle in May 1981 when the bodies of two Salvadorean refugees were found near the El Salvador–Honduras border. The resulting furore elicited a report from World Vision headquarters deploring 'a series of disconnected and random actions by many of our Honduran refugee relief staff that are inconsistent with our policies, our commitment to excellence, our Christian ethics and the local necessities and realities'. It is this history that still dogs World Vision; certainly it must be the only aid organization that in its official manifesto feels it necessary to deny any links with intelligence agencies: 'World Vision has not . . . does not . . . will not allow any of its staff knowingly to have any relationship with, obtain information from, or provide information to any intelligence service or agency whether private or governmental'.[65] However, many aid agencies now give it credit for radical changes, and it has internationalized its leadership.

There is a major difference between World Vision and other church relief and development agencies, and this is World Vision's missionary or evangelistic (in their terms 'holistic') stance. All the main-line church relief agencies were established precisely to separate humanitarian aid from mission work. A Lutheran relief worker, for instance, who tries to convert aid recipients is violating agency rules. But for World Vision workers,

---

[65] World Vision International, *Understanding Who We Are* (Monrovia CA, World Vision International, no date [available from WVI, 919 West Huntington Drive, Monrovia CA 91016, USA]), 12.

spreading Christianity is the reason for all projects. This mission is taken seriously: in the words of a Zimbabwean World Vision official, 'Even when digging a borehole, we are looking for opportunities to give the Word'. All projects will have an evangelization committee, made up of local people from local churches. To be sure, the official World Vision International manifesto insists that they 'by Board policy are opposed to proselytism or coercion of any kind',[66] but it is easy to see why field operatives can sometimes blur the distinction between giving something for evangelization, and giving something on condition that recipients are evangelized. Certainly, by World Vision's own admission, this is what happened in Central America in 1981.[67]

There is a suspicion that aid can sometimes be used the other way, too: crucial assistance can be suddenly terminated for anyone involved in social or political activity. In August 1985, fishermen and farmers of Iling Island in the Philippines addressed a letter to World Vision's main office protesting against the treatment of those among them who were associated with a locally-formed — and government-encouraged — organization called the Fraternity of Fishermen and Farmers. For those linked to the organization, children's sponsorship was terminated, medical aid denied, and typhoon relief aid refused.[68]

Also, World Vision is not a Church; and it 'does not have a structural affiliation with any Church or interchurch body'. Its links are

at the community level . . . These working relationships can be with a group of local churches; sometimes with a community committee on which the churches are represented; sometimes with a single congregation (though we prefer to work with a group of churches as an interchurch committee), and sometimes with a project committee of individual Christians.[69]

However, World Vision grew out of American evangelicalism. It has changed greatly since then, even its critics admit, and it has internationalized its leadership — its current chief executive is a Scot. But the churches it co-

[66] World Vision International, *Understanding Who We Are*, 8.

[67] Askin, 'Hostility, conflict engulf World Vision', 36.

[68] The letter bitterly attacks WVI for 'exploitation . . . paternalism, dependency, mendicancy [mendacity?] . . . insincerity . . . high-handed treatment . . . harrassment . . . deception'. The signatories state: 'We did not ask WV to come to our island . . . We never realized our poverty would be exploited . . . We are poor, now we have been made beggars'. The spokesman for the signatories was Revd Toribio Cajiuat, United Methodist Church, San Jose, Occidental Mindoro, Philippines.

[69] World Vision International, *Understanding Who We Are*, 11.

operates with at the project level tend to be the evangelical churches from which it grew, and while World Vision International has changed in one way, many of these churches have changed in accordance with the recent American revival. So, in practice, what is passed on as Christianity, through World Vision organization and World Vision funding, may not be the evangelicalism that the internationalized World Vision leaders adhere to at head office, but the American civil religion of the churches co-operating at grass roots.

World Vision came to Rhodesia, from South Africa, in 1969.[70] In 1979 it became autonomous as World Vision Zimbabwe (WVZ). It is now a big agency, employing about 50 from its Harare office, and another 50 out in the field. Since Independence it has thoroughly Africanized, and now this work-force is almost totally composed of Black Zimbabweans. World Vision has a policy of employing only Christians,[71] and all the Zimbabwean staff are evangelical Protestants. WVZ's work can be divided into six categories: child and family care, emergency aid, community development, church leadership enhancement, challenge to mission, and, most importantly, evangelism. This last is the most important because, as a WVZ official said, 'all our projects are vehicles through which the message of God comes to people'. For these projects, WVZ had a budget in 1986 of Z$2,5 million. This money comes directly from the head office in California, but it is raised in the United States, Canada, Australia, New Zealand, and Europe. In 1987, WVZ experienced some drop in funds, partly as a result of the drop in contributions caused by events like the Bakker scandal in America, partly because more of the available resources had been diverted to emergencies in Ethiopia. Development receives approximately three times the funds allocated to relief work. Development work encompasses everything from boreholes, clinics, grinding-mills, and pre-schools, to carpentry shops, weaving co-operatives, irrigation schemes, welding, and adult literacy. The relief assistance is mainly for Mozambique, and, within Zimbabwe, for the Mozambican refugee camps at Mazowe and Nyangombe. WVZ claims it has no problems dealing with a Marxist government, with whom relations are good.

[70] Interview with two WVZ officials, Harare, 3 Nov. 1987.
[71] World Vision International, *Understanding Who We Are*, 14.

Christ for All Nations (CfAN)

CfAN has conducted three revivals in Zimbabwe since Independence in 1980. In May 1986, CfAN staged its third crusade in conjunction with a Fire Conference for evangelists from all over Africa. This Fire Conference drew 4 000 delegates from 41 African countries. The Christianity of both the crusade and the conference was American evangelicalism. This was obvious from the bookshop, where the following booklets were on sale: twelve titles by Jimmy Swaggart; eighteen by Kenneth E. Hagin, the founder of Rhema Bible Church; three by Ray McCauley, who founded Rhema in South Africa; eleven by Kenneth and Gloria Copeland, both promoters of the gospel of prosperity, and the former the promoter of South Africa in 'The Other South Africa' video; seven by Gordon Lindsay, the founder of Christ For The Nations in Dallas, Texas; five by Elijah Maswanganyi of South Africa; three by John Osteen of Lakewood International Outreach Church, Houston, Texas. Apart from these there were only another thirteen miscellaneous titles on sale.[72]

This conclusion is reinforced by listing the main speakers. Bonnke apart, the five most influential leaders of the Fire Conference seminars were from the southern states of America or from California. These were Loren Cunningham of YWAM; both the Copelands; Ralph Mahoney, of World Missionary Assistance Plan, California; and Wayne Meyers, now of Mexico. Other key speakers I have already had occasion to mention were Ray McCauley of Rhema, and Ed Roebert of Hatfield Christian Church in Pretoria.

Not surprisingly, since the events were being held in Zimbabwe, overt displays of anti-communism and anti-socialism were rare. However, these sentiments surfaced occasionally. 'The Church can stop Marxism, communism and bad politicians', declared Benson Idahosa of Nigeria, another of the main speakers.[73] As well, Idahosa saw divine providence behind Reagan's America:

The Holy Spirit can change the power of government in any nation. For many years America had weak Presidents. A few years ago American Christians gathered together and said "Washington for Jesus! Washington for Jesus!" and they proclaimed the gospel in Washington. After a few months they had an election, and a new President ... After that election, things began to change. The power of God came back on things.[74]

---

[72] For a full discussion of this and the following points, see Gifford, ' "Africa shall be saved" ', 63–92.
[73] Sermon delivered at CfAN crusade, Harare, 26 April 1986.   [74] Ibid.

68

Mainly, however, the attitude to politics is 'leave it alone'. Thus, Idahosa again:

I don't believe in political priests and bishops. I believe in signs and wonders in the name of Jesus. All you in South Africa, you need a ministry of signs and wonders. The USA will not solve your problems. Britain will not solve your problems. Russia will not solve your problems. Signs and wonders will solve your problems.[75]

But even when the anti-communism is not overt, even when the 'hands off politics' message is not explicit, this Christianity still plays a political role. As I have noted elsewhere, by focusing so narrowly on supernatural causes, it diverts attention from the economic or political causes of so much reality — it hardly encourages critical analyses of the economic interests or forces shaping society. By advocating the gospel of prosperity, it dissuades adherents from evaluating the present economic order, merely persuading them to try to be among those who benefit from it. With its emphasis on personal healing, it diverts attention from social ills that are crying out for remedy. Its stress on human wickedness and the 'fallen' nature of 'the world' is no incentive to social, economic or constitutional reform. By emphasizing personal morality so exclusively, it all but eliminates any interest in systemic or institutionalized injustice. By making everything so simple, it distracts attention from the very real contradictions in the lives of so many in Southern Africa. By spiritualizing everything, it leaves no room for social involvement, except that of exerting influence by the example of personal holiness. The whole package is a vote for the status quo.[76]

That at least some of the speakers were hiding their full political agenda became evident soon afterwards, when Ralph Mahoney, on his return to the United States, published in his magazine a blistering attack on Zimbabwe, describing it as a communist tyranny, in contrast to South Africa which was described as an embattled democracy.[77] Of Zimbabwe he wrote:

The nation became the object of communist interest some fifteen years ago,

---

[75] Ibid.

[76] See Gifford, ' "Africa shall be saved" ', 86.

[77] The whole article is found in Mahoney's *World MAP Digest*, 1987, 12–15. It drew a response (dated 9 Mar. 1987) from twelve evangelical pastors who had been involved in the Fire Conference, who said that unless Mahoney apologized they would have no option but to refuse co-operation to missionary personnel and organizations holding such views. Part of the original article and evangelists' response is found in the *Herald* (19 Mar. 1987), 4. (While in Harare, Mahoney had been guest preacher at the Christian Life Centre.)

resulting in a 10-year civil war. The war ended tragically when the leaders of Rhodesia were betrayed by US Government State Department leaders.

Other western nations broke their promises as well, and the struggling white minority could not hold out against the betrayal. A Marxist (communist) government came to power and now rules the nation.

Today, anti-American slogans and rhetoric spew non-stop from the radio stations, newspapers and television.

Then he catalogued Zimbabwe's evils — corruption, communist dictator, mismanagement, police and military abuse. 'The only bright side to this desperate situation is this. In the midst of chaotic upheaval, and despotic terror being spread by the current governments of Africa, the Holy Spirit is at work.' Bonnke is calling to the church to save Africa: 'Would the Church and should the Church respond to this call — God would intervene and turn back the communist threat which is sinking the ship called Africa!' And then the 'true story' about South Africa:

> If we continue to swallow the communist propaganda and believe the simplistic thesis that Africa's complex problems will be solved by destroying the only viable, prosperous capitalist country on the continent [South Africa], we shall see the greatest human tragedy in human history unfold before the year 2000.
>
> South Africa is under siege now by communists. And our Western nations abandoning [sic] the peoples of South Africa but in fact contributing to the downfall of this one prosperous stable democracy.

Mahoney's conclusion is the hope that the peoples of Africa find Jesus Christ sufficient for them: ' "God save Africa" is our prayer! May its peoples find the reality of Jesus Christ in the saving grace of God sufficient for their desperate needs. "Africa shall be saved!" God grant it be so!'

It is clear from what and for whom CfAN wants Africa saved.

Rhema Bible Church

Rhema Bible Church held its first service in Zimbabwe in April 1982, with six people in the pastor's home.[78] It now meets in the Harry Margolis Hall, Harare, with 600 adults and 175 children attending Sunday morning service, and 300 adults attending the evening service (though about 150 believers attend both services). It has 475 full partners as members, which involves attending the Wednesday night 'Care Groups', commitment in 'outreach', and tithing. Of the adherents, about 20 per cent are Black.

---

[78] Interview with founder-pastor, Harare, 19 Aug. 1987.

Today, Rhema has sixteen full-time employees. It claims to run two Bible schools, audio- and videotape ministries, a prison ministry, a youth ministry (of 150), a hospital ministry, a radio ministry, and Compassion Ministries, its relief arm in Zimbabwe's four major refugee camps. It also sees itself as called to work in 'the five nations of Central Africa'.

The pastor describes the church as belonging properly to the 'Word of Faith Movement', a section of the charismatic movement. Its statement of faith expresses belief in, among other things: the Scriptures as 'our infallible guide in matters pertaining to conduct and doctrine . . . ; baptism in water . . . by immersion . . . for believers only'; baptism in the Holy Spirit for believers, accompanied by speaking in tongues; physical healing as the privilege of every member of the Church today; the imminent return of Jesus; the rapture and the millennial reign after tribulation; a literal lake of fire, in which 'one who physically dies in his sins without Christ is hopelessly and eternally lost'.[79]

Rhema is a classic example of American evangelicalism, as is obvious to anyone attending its services. Its use of the Bible is strictly fundamentalist, as seen in its dismissal of evolution, for example. The gospel of prosperity is unmistakable; the message is insistent that health and prosperity are the right of every true Christian, so much so that poverty and disease manifest a deficient Christian life. There is great stress on obedience. All full members are required to attend the cell groups ('Care Groups') every Wednesday evening. All these strands are crucial in the new American evangelicalism.

But the links with American evangelicalism are more specific than this. The founder and pastor of Rhema in Zimbabwe studied for two years under Gordon Lindsay at Christ For The Nations, Dallas, Texas. (Gordon Lindsay was a fundamentalist and dispensationalist whose reading of the Bible, as we shall see, was as 'imaginative' as Hal Lindsey's *Late Great Planet Earth*.) The two Bible schools run by Rhema use a Bible course devised in 1974 by Kenneth Hagin, the founder of Rhema Bible Church in Tulsa, Oklahoma, and one of the prime exponents of the gospel of prosperity. Jimmy Swaggart's booklets dominate the Rhema book-racks (and the director of Jimmy Swaggart Ministries in Zimbabwe used to be Rhema's business manager; he still attends Rhema, with two of the other three Harare

---

[79] Available from Rhema Bible Church, P. O. Box M17, Mabelreign, Harare.

staff of Jimmy Swaggart Ministries). Rhema's Compassion Ministries has received aid — 81 tons of rice, 20 tons of wheat — shipped and paid for by Pat Robertson's Operation Blessing. (Pat Robertson, it will be remembered, supports the Contras and gives such humanitarian aid in Nicaragua.) Rhema's audio- and videotape collections feature almost exclusively the big names of American evangelicalism. This is the Christianity of the Deep South.

Just as important as these links with the American South is the considerable influence Rhema has on Zimbabwe's Christianity generally. Rhema itself plants other churches, already about twelve: for example, it has established churches in refugee camps, at Mazowe, and three at Wedza of about 150 members each. Rhema establishes them and gives them six months' finance and support. These churches are called simply 'Christian' and autonomous, but the brand of Christianity is, naturally enough, Rhema's. However, besides that, Rhema has a wide influence through its links with other churches. It has close links with the King's Church and the Christian Life Centre. Rhema took a prominent part in the 1986 CfAN crusade. Rhema pastors teach at Bishop Guti's Africa Multination for Christ Institute, Zimbabwe's biggest Bible college. It has close links with Andrew Wutawanashe, pastor of the Family of God Church; much of the literature used in the refugee camps was written by Wutawanashe. Rhema works closely with Africa Enterprise; at least one of Rhema's pastors works in Africa Enterprise's 'Go Teams' (groups of three who witness in homes or at work) and in the refugee camps Rhema uses Africa Enterprise's 'Fox Fires' (young Bible-college students who operate in pairs in a rural ministry). The director for sub-Saharan Africa of the Morris Cerullo World Evangelism organization attends the Rhema Church. I have already mentioned Rhema's close links with Jimmy Swaggart Ministries in Zimbabwe. Above all, though, Rhema exerts wide influence through its education of Zimbabwean ministers. Rhema is run by three elders, its three pastors. Two of these, along with the pastor of Bulawayo's Christian Centre, comprise the three directors of the Africa Fellowship of Christian Ministers. This Fellowship exists for leaders in ministry, most of whom are pastors. It meets for two days every two months; it has fifty official members, but it can have up to 120 at these assemblies. In mid-1986, these pastors attended a retreat conducted by Pastor Willie Crewe of Hatfield Christian Church in Pretoria, which I have had occasion to mention before. The meeting in

November 1987, attended by 120 from all over the country, was addressed by Ray McCauley, who just happened to be visiting Zimbabwe; McCauley, whom we have also met before, is the founder of Rhema in South Africa. In June 1988 they were addressed on the topic of money by Californian fundamentalist Ed Cole, a proponent of the gospel of prosperity and author of booklets like *Invest to Increase: Ten Basics for Investment of your Time, Talent, Treasure*.[80] All these links are channels through which Rhema spreads its brand of Christianity.

It is not claimed here that Rhema personnel are motivated by any sinister intent, but I have already noted in the case of Nicaragua the political role of schemes for educating local pastors.

The Unification Church (Moonies)

In one sense, the Unification Church does not belong in these pages. Whereas nearly all the organizations of the religious right see one another as partners, and readily co-operate to achieve their goals, many of them would categorically deny the title 'Christian' to the Moonies, because their founder, Moon, considers himself the new Messiah. But in another sense the Unification Church does belong with the other organizations we have considered here, for the forces which have fostered the religious right generally are the very factors which explain the rise of Moon's empire. Also, the identity of at least some of their aims has led to considerable, if sometimes embarrassed, co-operation between the religious right and Moon.[81]

The Moonies make up a politico-religious empire with an annual profit of well over half a billion dollars, placing it in the top fifty of the world's largest private companies. One well-informed estimate puts the Church's 1984 profits as high as US$700 million — roughly equal to Toyota's, and

---

[80] E. L. Cole, *Invest to Increase: Ten Basics for Investment of your Time, Talent, Treasure* (Tulsa OK, Harrison House, 1988). Cole gave public seminars at the Harare Sheraton, 22–25 June, and at the Bulawayo Sun Hotel, 29 June – 2 July 1988. The headquarters of Cole's numerous ministries are in Dallas (Box 610588, Dallas TX 75261, USA).

[81] For an exhaustive discussion of the Moon phenomenon, see J-F. Boyer, *L'Empire Moon* (Paris, La Découverte, 1986). Unless indicated to the contrary, all the details following are found in R. W. Johnson, 'Rising Moon', *London Review of Books* (18 Dec. 1986), 3–6, which is a review of Boyer's book. For Moon's activities in Latin America, see J-F. Boyer and A. Alem, 'The Moonies — a power in the service of anticommunism', *Guardian Weekly* (24 Feb. 1985), 12–13; and 'Moon in Latin America: Building the bases of a world organization', *Guardian Weekly* (3 Mar. 1985), 12, 14 [articles originally published in *Le Monde diplomatique* (Feb. 1985)].

more than those of Unilever, International Telephone and Telegraph Corporation (ITT) or Chrysler.[82] Its founder, Sun Myung Moon, is a Korean who has lived through and been formed by the Japanese occupation of Korea, the Japanese defeat, and the Korean War. Straight after the Second World War, Moon proclaimed himself the Messiah (one of over a hundred in Korea this century), and in May 1954 he founded his Unification Church. From the beginning he directed his attention towards the military. He was associated with high-ranking military officers who rose to influence in the 1961 coup which brought President Park to power, and who, with the help of the CIA, set up the South Korean KCIA which from that day to this has remained the real power in Korea. Four of these original KCIA figures are today at the summit of the Moonie movement. This is the origin of the fanatical anti-communism of the Moonies ('Some say that communism is soluble in Coca-Cola, but it is only soluble in napalm'). Within a very short time, the Moonies' links with the Korean political–military–intelligence world were so close that it was hard to know where the South Korean government ended and the Moonies began.

Financially, they flourished from the beginning. Money came not only from the unpaid labour of adherents, but from a growing ring of Moonie enterprises. The first, significantly, was a gun factory, and soon the Moonies had a key role in the Korean defence industry. Soon they were making, under American franchise, the M16 assault-rifle, the M60 machine-gun, the M79 grenade-launcher, the Vulcan anti-aircraft gun, and much more. (The British attaché in Seoul in 1985 claimed that he had a two-page list of Moonie companies working in the Korean defence industry.) Since those first years, they have branched out into agricultural machinery, machine tools, the titanium industry, pharmaceuticals, fishing, the import–export business, printing, steel, agricultural products and banking. By 1985, there were 118 such companies in the USA alone. Often enough there have been tax scandals attached to these firms, for the Moonies seem to feel that none of their operations should have to pay tax at all.

Moon also came to receive considerable funds from the American far right, and in 1970 he transferred his base to the USA where he has since focused his activities. Right from the beginning he courted the Washington establishment. Before long he had the willing patronage of a host of

---

[82] Boyer and Alem, 'The Moonies', 12.

important figures, and Nixon, grateful for Moon's unstinting support during Watergate, even invited Moon to the White House where the two men prayed together. Nixon's fall, a serious blow for Moon, saw Moon redouble his efforts to counter the left and to rally the right. His newspaper *Rising Tide* played a large part in this, and he went on to launch his own New York *News World* to counter the *New York Times* and in 1982 he joined a similar battle with the *Washington Post* by launching the Moonie *Washington Times*.

In the mid-1970s he began to suffer serious reverses. The hearings of the Congressional Sub-Committee on Korean–American Relations ('Korea-gate') uncovered an incredible array of KCIA attempts to use Moonies for all kinds of interference in American political life. Tax problems grew — these were to culminate in Moon's gaol sentence for tax evasion in 1984. At the same time anguished parents accused Moon of stealing and brain-washing their children. Several Moonies defected, telling horror stories of the sect's under-cover life. More importantly, the Moonies' cover was broken, and the full list of front organizations was exposed.

Yet the damage was not irreparable. On the contrary, Moon's influence was to become greater. The key was Reagan's election in 1980, to which Moon had committed his immense resources. Reagan appeared on election night proudly brandishing the Moonie *News World* heralding his victory. Moon was invited as a VIP to Reagan's inauguration. The *Washington Times* rapidly became the focus of the new and unparalleled Moonie influence. It rapidly became the preferred house magazine of the Reagan Administration. Reagan himself frequently told audiences to read the Moonie paper, and he gave it his first exclusive interview of his second term. The paper has taken the hardest line on every issue, being anti-détente, anti-arms control, pro-Contra (for whom it launched a massive private funding drive) and pro-South Africa. At the end of 1984, Reagan recruited Pat Buchanan, one of its leader writers, to become his main speech writer. Soon Buchanan ranked second only to Don Regan on the White House staff. Even Moon must have been staggered at his achievement.

Moon's ambitions reach beyond the United States. He has said, 'If we can manipulate at least seven nations, we'll control the whole world . . . In the camp of God, Korea, Japan, America, England, France, Germany and Italy are the nations on which I count in order to conquer the world'. His involvement in Latin America is considerable. Moon's deputy, Bo Hi Pak, has called Paraguay's dictator, General Stroessner, 'a special man, elected by God to rule his country'. There is some evidence that Moonies collaborated with Klaus Barbie to organize the 1980 Bolivian coup. In Chile, Pinochet has been accorded the honour of being classed with Moon himself as 'a pillar of the struggle against international Communism'. In Honduras, US$5 million of Moon's money went into the plotting which saw General Alvarez dismissed and sent into exile on 31 March 1984.[83] In Japan, where Moon has wide support and has drawn enormous funds, he is linked with former Prime Ministers Nakasone and Kishi (the latter a prominent war criminal), Kodama (the head of Japanese organized crime) and Sasakawa (an extremely rich war-time leader and Class A war criminal).[84] In France, according to Le Pen's estranged wife, Moon is an important financier of the National Front.[85]

Moon's relationship to the religious right has been highly controversial within the religious right itself. It is Moon's claim to be the new Messiah which is the main problem — one might well have thought it an insuperable problem. Also, Moon can be quite anti-American: he has called 'American-style democracy a good nursery for the growth of communism'.[86] He has also said, 'In the ideal world centred upon God everyone will speak only Korean'.[87] Probably, his less than total commitment to America is not so well known to members of the religious right. Certainly there are links between Moon and Tim LaHaye, and with the Coalition for Religious Freedom, with Jerry Falwell (who cut short his South African tour to appear at the banquet celebrating Moon's release from prison), and with Christian Voice.[88] Bo Hi Pak, Moon's deputy, has commented, 'This extraordinary match [between the religious right and Moon] shows what a great sense of humour God has'.[89]

Moon probably exerts most influence through his front organizations, many of which have titles high-sounding enough to deceive even the wary. Besides the Unification Church, the following organizations belong to the Moon constellation: American Youth for a Just Peace; The Association for the Progress of Honduras; the Confederation of Associations for the Unity

[83] A. S. Banks (ed.), *Political Handbook of the World, 1984–85* (Binghamton NY, CSA Publications, 1985), 216.
[84] F. Clarkson, 'Moon's law: God is phasing out democracy', *Covert Action Information Bulletin* (Spring 1987), 36, 43.
[85] Ibid., 40.
[86] Ibid., 38.
[87] Ibid., 39–40.
[88] Ibid., 44–5.
[89] *Newsweek* (15 Feb. 1988), 29.

of Societies of the Americas (CAUSA — the political wing of the Unification Church); the Freedom Leadership Foundation; The American Freedom Coalition; The Korean Cultural and Freedom Foundation; The Conference on the Unity of the Sciences (an organization sponsoring lavish all-expenses-paid conferences for academics); the World Media Association (which does the same for journalists). The Moon organization is an integral part of the very influential World Anti-Communist League (WACL) — in Japan, the leadership of WACL is almost identical with that of the Unification Church. All these bodies promote the Moonie aims. These aims are also promoted by the Moonie press: *Rising Tide*, the New York *News World* (later *New York Tribune*), the *Washington Times*, the *Washington Inquirer* (a weekly tabloid), and *Insight* (patterned on *Time* and *Newsweek*). Through fronts like these, Moon has even received the blessing of the Catholic Church, which in Latin America is normally very hostile to him. Because of this grass-roots opposition, Moon directed his attention to Rome itself. In Rome he established in 1984 a unit called the Association for the Unification of Latin America (AULA). AULA's second conference in December 1985 was attended by a dozen former Presidents of Latin American countries and the participants were received by the Pope.[90]

The Moonies began in Rhodesia in 1976, holding their first meeting in Salisbury on 17 September of that year.[91] Their growth was most marked between Independence and September 1985, during which time there seemed to be a steady increase in adherents. They have formed communes in the Harare suburbs of Belgravia and Alexandra Park, and have a farm at Ruwa, near Harare. There were about 200 adherents in Zimbabwe in 1987. Their leader in Zimbabwe, a Japanese, has banned members from watching television programmes supporting the government, forbidden their joining political parties, denounced the President and Prime Minister as communists, and forbidden any association with the national flag (because of its red star). Alarmed by reports of these things, and by reports of Moonie activities overseas, the Zimbabwe government suspended all Moonie activities in 1986, but they continued to operate secretly in Mount Pleasant, Harare. In 1986 they also attempted to open a branch church in Mutare.

The Moonies operate through a front organization, a registered commer-

[90] Clarkson, 'Moon's law', 46.
[91] The following details are taken from a Zimbabwe Inter-Africa News Agency press release dated 29 September 1987, most of which comprised statements made in the sworn affidavit of a former member.

cial enterprise, through which they attempt to foster contacts with government officials. In mid-1987 a Zimbabwean newspaper showed the chairman of this front company, which operates under a Shona name, making a donation to the Prime Minister for the Zimbabwean troops guarding the Beira Corridor, and also towards the new party headquarters being built in Harare, and for the Non-Aligned Movement of which Mugabe is the current chairman. Some prominent academics at the University of Zimbabwe have been on Moonie-sponsored study tours and attended Moonie conferences.

Moon's links with Zimbabwe were highlighted in March 1988 in a rather bizarre way. It was reported that Moon's son, Heung Jin Nim, killed in a car crash in 1984 when aged seventeen, had become reincarnated in a young Zimbabwean. The Zimbabwean was unnamed, but said to be Black, baby-faced, in his mid-twenties, of medium build, with a perfect command of English and a booming laugh. He had been a member of the Unification Church for three years when he began to make claims to hear the voice of Heung Jin Nim. A high Church official flew to Zimbabwe to investigate, bringing from Moon five questions which only Moon's son could answer. The Zimbabwean is reported to have answered them perfectly, and was taken to the United States where Moon enthusiastically accepted him as his son. The Zimbabwean assumed the name of Heung Jin Nim, and soon left on a tour of Europe, the United States and South Korea, preaching and presiding over church ceremonies of confession, admonishing believers about their sins. In these sessions, he is alleged to be rather physical, and reports have circulated that the hospitalization in December 1987 of Moon's deputy, Bo Hi Pak, was a result of being physically admonished by the Zimbabwean. Some members have hailed this alleged reincarnation as the most momentous event in the Church's history. Other associates of Moon's have been decidedly uncomfortable, one even suggesting that because of Zimbabwe's links with North Korea, the Zimbabwean is probably a North Korean 'plant' designed to discredit Moon and his anti-communist crusade.[92]

The Unification Church in Zimbabwe is under a regional office in Zambia, which also controls their operations in Malawi, Mozambique, Angola and Tanzania. Johannesburg has another office, responsible for South Africa, Botswana, Namibia, Swaziland and Lesotho. An office in Nairobi is responsible for East African countries.

[92] *San Francisco Chronicle* (30 Mar 1988), A8; *Newsweek* (11 Apr. 1988), 27.

The organizations we have considered above (leaving aside the Unification Church) are examples of churches or ministries, of varying size and influence, which promote a particular brand of Christianity. They would all tend to call it 'Christianity' *tout court*, implicitly— sometimes explicitly— denying that label to mainstream denominations. This, however, is too simple. The Christianity they promote is of a very particular type — recent, fundamentalist in theology, privatized and politically conservative. It is part of an American cultural phenomenon, and the links are obvious from their parent bodies, the books they use, their tapes and music, sometimes their funding, often their pastors.

But these religious transnationals and their subsidiaries are not the only promoters of this kind of Christianity. Zimbabwe has witnessed a mushrooming of small, private ministries, products of the same social, cultural and political forces. They, too, propagate the same brand of Christianity. As an example of these ministries, consider Shekinah Ministries, an off-shoot of Chipinge's White Assemblies of God Church. The President of Shekinah is a White Zimbabwean Assemblies of God pastor. Shekinah reduces the political situation in Southern Africa to its most basic religious form. In a letter dated 15 February 1985, it is stated:

The situation [in Mozambique] is as follows:
1) Mozambique is under legal control of an anti-Christian government.
2) The Renamo [or MNR] forces are fighting communism . . .
3) There are truly two governments in one nation. The Renamo are a real army with efficient military structure. They are not a bunch of bandits. They are trained soldiers.
4) We believe that it won't be long before Renamo are in full control of Mozambique, two years at the most.

The same letter recounts how Shekinah's President, Michael Howard, and two colleagues deliberately went into Renamo territory, hoping to be kidnapped. They were captured, explained they had come 'to preach to them at the risk of our lives . . . What a reward we had when we preached to the commander and saw him and his friend take off their hats and kneel in the dust accepting Jesus the very first day after our capture'. This caused such a stir that their 'highest ranking officer . . . came after a week walking 300 kilometres to see us . . . The Renamo soldiers accepted us totally . . . and told us we were free, but we were not satisfied to leave things as [*sic*] that. We asked if we could see their President, Alfonso Dhlakama. They agreed to take us to him at their headquarters only 30 to 40 days journey by foot'. Dhlakama, the letter claims, said, 'We need God, we want Jesus'.[93]

Shekinah, although a local body, obviously sees itself as part of the particular American religious scene we have been discussing. The letter was distributed to US churches, appealing for funds. The Believers' Church, Coalinga, was one of those that took up the appeal. Again, note the simplistic dualism of the Coalinga pastor: 'Renamo is a group seeking to overthrow Marxist forces governing Mozambique — tough, professional guerrilla forces originating in South Africa, and presently controlling over half the country. Ministry is now secured in any area they control. "We want God — We want Jesus — Send us Bibles", they are saying, and Shekinah is seeking to comply post-haste'. This pastor calls for funds ('revival fires are burning hot') and announces that he is going to Zimbabwe (13–31 May 1985) to videotape Shekinah's ministry, and to go on his own preaching mission to [Renamo-held areas of?] Mozambique.[94] Shekinah's American links are further obvious from the fact that a group called the End-Time Handmaidens of Jasper, Arkansas, has come to Zimbabwe to help Shekinah. Shekinah has links with Gordon Lindsay's Christ For The Nations in Dallas, Texas; in 1987, Christ For The Nations spent US$9 691 on a van for Shekinah.[95] A group called Don Normand Ministries of Florida circulates newsletters from and raises funds for Shekinah.[96] Shekinah also has links with the American mercenaries' magazine, Soldier of Fortune.[97] The US links are evident, too, from Shekinah's request for coverage on the Bakkers' PTL programme or Robertson's 700 Club in mid-1985.[98]

The exact nature of Shekinah's activities in Mozambique became evident at the trial of a Shekinah missionary to Mozambique. On 23 March 1988, Ian Grey, a 27-year-old Australian, was sentenced by a military

[93] Letter sent out by Believers' Church, P. O. Box 437, Coalinga CA 93210, USA.
[94] Undated appeal of pastor of Believers' Church; see previous footnote.
[95] A review of 1987 expenses in Christ For The Nations, Dec. 1987, mentions the money for a van for Mozambique missionaries. That the missionaries were from Shekinah was verified by personal communication. (Christ For The Nations, as we have seen, is where the founder of Rhema in Zimbabwe studied; another former student of Christ For The Nations runs Africa for Christ in Gweru (P. O. Box 745, Gweru, Zimbabwe; he also gives an address in Dallas, Texas), which began its own Bible college in 1987 with nine students; and Gordon Lindsay's booklets, as we shall see below, are given mass distribution in Zimbabwe by Global Literature Lifeline.)
[96] Personal letter dated 11 December 1987 from Don Normand Ministries Inc., P. O. Box 813, Melrose FL 32666, USA.
[97] See Mozambique Information Agency (AIM) despatch No. 141 (Apr. 1988), 7.
[98] Letter dated 14 January 1985; also sent out by Believers' Church; see footnote 93.

80

tribunal to ten and a half years in prison on various counts, including collaboration with Renamo. He had been arrested on 2 November 1987 while crossing from Malawi to Zimbabwe through Mozambique. In the months before his trial the Renamo office in Washington claimed he was being tortured, charges which were given much publicity in Australia and South Africa, and hundreds of letters of protest flooded into Maputo from fundamentalist churches in the United States. A few days after his conviction, Grey gave an account of his activities to a major Australian newspaper. He denied that he had been maltreated in prison, and apologized for the harm he had done to the people of Mozambique. He explained that in 1986 he had been in Israel, and had undergone a religious experience. Soon after, in Tel Aviv, he had been recruited by Shekinah's Michael Howard 'to do the Lord's work' in Mozambique, by working in Renamo-held areas. He had been persuaded that by working with the rebels he could help spread Christianity in the country. He had been based in Malawi, but had often entered Mozambique illegally. He freely admitted that his work had helped fund-raising for weapons in the United States. He admitted that he had been given information on Renamo activities and Frelimo troop movements, and had telephoned this information from Malawi to Renamo spokesman in Washington, Tom Schaaf. (Schaaf himself had previously been a missionary with Mission to Mozambique in Mutare.)[99] Grey described himself as 'an MNR messenger boy'. He said,

> I was naïve, foolish, and was a tool of those who committed horrendous acts against the Mozambican people ... I was duped by political Christians into believing that the MNR were freedom fighters and churches were being destroyed ... When I heard from my father [who had come from Australia to attend the trial] that there was religious freedom and more churches now than when Frelimo took over at independence from Portugal in 1975, I realised how I had been duped ...
> 'I saw a lot of suffering in the areas I preached. Some had only bark for clothing. But today I realise the only way to change that is to get rid of the MNR. Without

---

[99] This is another instance of a missionary with definite links with the (anti-communist and therefore godly) MNR. In 1985, Thomas Schaaf, an agricultural extension worker and member of Mission to Mozambique, an off-shoot of Mutare's charismatic One Way Christian Centre, left the country only to appear in Washington DC, as spokesman for the MNR. The One Way pastor, Duane Udd, in 1986 issued a statement dissociating the church from Schaaf and said his church is totally apolitical. Despite some police enquiries about Schaaf, Udd said his Church's evangelization and medical work in Mozambique carries on unhindered; see Askin, 'Is religious freedom misused?', 9.

South African support, and *the support of people in the United States who back organisations like Shekinah*, I do not believe the MNR could survive.'[100]

After Shekinah's activities were mentioned in an article in *Moto*, Howard closed down Shekinah in Zimbabwe and moved his entire operation to Malawi in December 1987.[101]

In this section we have considered some organizations which propagate a recent American brand of Christianity, which, whether adherents are aware of it or not, performs a particular social and political function. We now turn to a more theoretical discussion of different kinds of Christianity.

---

[100] *Sydney Morning Herald* (28 Mar. 1988), 1, 13, emphasis added; see also *Bulletin* [Sydney] (12 Apr. 1988), 37. The source for the allegations of torture was apparently Peter Hammond, the director of Frontline Fellowship (P. O. Box 74, Newlands 7725, South Africa). Hammond actually told the BBC that the Australian High Commissioner in Harare had told him that Grey had been tortured, a claim the High Commissioner promptly denied, adding that he had never even spoken to Hammond; see Mozambique Information Agency (AIM) despatch No. 141 (Apr. 1988), 6. Hammond's pro-Unita, pro-Renamo *Frontline Fellowship News* comprises such 'reports' of 'Marxist atrocities' in Mozambique and Angola. Grey was sentenced just before a report prepared for the US Department of State made public the scale of MNR atrocities: the report estimates MNR 'murders' at about 100 000. R. Gersony, 'Summary of Mozambican Refugee Accounts of Principally Conflict-Related Experiences in Mozambique: Report Submitted to Ambassador Jonathan Moore, Director, Bureau for Refugee Programs, and Dr Chester A. Crocker, Assistant Secretary for African Affairs' (Washington, unpubl. mimeo., 1988), 25.

[101] Askin, 'Is religious freedom misused?', 9; see also *Herald* (7 Jan. 1988), 5.

4 Two Kinds of Christianity

It is clear that religion can play one of two roles in society, depending on the form it takes. Baum has called these two forms of religion 'utopian' and 'ideological'. Ideological religion legitimates the existing social order, defends the dominant values, enhances the authority of the dominant group, and is calculated to preserve the existing society. Utopian religion, however, reveals the limitations of the existing social order, questions the dominant values of society, challenges the authority of the dominant group, and seeks to improve the current social order.[1]

It is probably true that religion of its nature tends to be, in Baum's terms, ideological. Religions of their nature tend to give great weight to stability, order, tradition, permanence, authority. That this has been so is evident from history. The history of all religions shows just how supportive of the status quo religion is. Romans of the first century AD still formally and publicly practised a religion which used flint knives in its sacrificial cult. When metal knives had come into use centuries before, the rest of society moved on, but religion maintained the old practice. The Jewish Passover has always been celebrated with unleavened bread, probably because the religious ritual goes back to a period before leaven had come into use.[2] The Stowe Missal shows that in the ninth century the Irish Church was still in its liturgy praying for 'the two emperors and their armies', even though there had been only one emperor for over three hundred years. Those Anglicans who use the 1662 Prayer Book still pray at their communion service for the governing

---

[1] Baum, *Religion and Alienation*, 102–3. Baum is here building on Karl Mannheim. Like most typologies, Baum's oversimplifies, but it serves our purpose here, without excessive distortion. For a more elaborate categorization of various kinds of Christianity, see A. Dulles, *Models of the Church* (New York, Doubleday, 1974).

[2] M. Noth, *Exodus* (Philadelphia, Westminster Press, 1962 [German original, 1959]), 89, 98–9.

authorities of England as they existed in Elizabethan times; they pray for the Queen and her Privy Council, making no mention of Parliament, Cabinet or Prime Minister.[3] The Catholic Church until very recently used a language which had not been spoken for centuries, and still uses vestments which are simply stylized versions of the clothing of even older times.

Nor are these examples just accidents of history. Sociologically, religions can be described as 'social organizations for universe maintenance'. That is, they preserve the cohesion of a society, neutralize forces of disintegration, maintain a society's perceptions and values, by providing an overall framework which can explain everything that happens within a society. In this way they validate accepted attitudes and received conceptions, and resist innovations. Berger and Luckmann write:

> It should not surprise us, then, that a profound affinity exists between those with an interest in maintaining established power positions and the personnel administering monopolistic traditions of universe-maintenance. In other words, conservative political forces tend to support the monopolistic claims of the universal experts whose monopolistic organizations in turn tend to be politically conservative. Historically, of course, most of these monopolies have been religious. It is thus possible to say that churches, understood as monopolistic combinations of full-time experts in a religious definition of reality, are inherently conservative once they have succeeded in establishing their monopoly in a given society. Conversely, ruling groups with a stake in the maintenance of the political status quo are inherently churchly in their religious orientation and, by the same token, suspicious of all innovations in the religious tradition.[4]

So religion tends to cement and uphold existing structures, to act as a conservative force. Many would hold that religion can be only of this kind, perpetuating man-made structures and ideologies which benefit those in power and keep the masses in their place. This is the understanding popularly attributed to Marx: that religion must be, can only be, an opiate to keep the masses subservient. This understanding lies behind Nietzsche's contempt for Christians for 'crouching to the cross', for glorying in their suffering and seeing it as God-given, rather than seeing it as inflicted on them by the powerful and resisting it.[5] That religion may be — even tends

[3] J. Daniélou, A. H. Couratin and J. Kent, *Historical Theology* (Harmondsworth, Penguin, Pelican Guide to Modern Theology 2, 1969), 19.

[4] P. L. Berger and T. Luckmann, *The Social Construction of Reality* (Harmondsworth, Penguin, 1967), 140.

[5] See discussion in H. Küng, *On Being a Christian* (London, Collins, 1978 [German original, 1974]), 571–3.

to be — ideological and may play a key role in perpetuating oppression cannot be denied.

A classic example of ideological religion was to be found in the southern part of Africa in the Portuguese colonies of Angola and Mozambique. In 1940 the Catholic Church entered into a concordat with Lisbon. In return for considerable financial help (salaries — for a bishop, the salary of a Governor — pensions, free travel, tax concessions), a privileged position, and permission to introduce some non-Portuguese missionaries, the Catholic Church merged its work with that of colonization. It was actually stated in law that the Catholic missions were 'instruments of civilization and national influence' (Colonial Act, 1940) and that 'the Portuguese Catholic Missions are considered to be institutions of imperial utility' (Missionary Statute, 1941). The Catholic Church thus became a tool in the Portugalization of millions of Africans, even consenting to be told what language it must use in instruction, and what kind of education could be given. As the Portuguese administration came to be seen as ever more oppressive, the Catholic Church came to be deeply compromised. Some missionaries called for the Catholic authorities to declare unequivocally whose side they were on. The bishops remained silent. The missionaries belonging to the Catholic congregation of the White Fathers then chose to withdraw from Mozambique altogether rather than be seen to be part of the system of oppression.

In their final statement they declared:

For a long time we waited for the [Catholic] hierarchy to take a definite stand to dispel these ambiguities in the face of injustice and police brutality. Faced with a silence we do not understand, we feel in conscience that we have not the right to be accounted the accomplices of an official support which the Bishops in this way seem to give to a regime which shrewdly uses the Church to consolidate and perpetuate in Africa an anachronistic situation.[6]

When this decision was made public these missionaries were expelled by orders of the special political police (DGS) at forty-eight hours notice. The last of them left on 30 May 1971. The Catholic bishops remained mute, not only in the face of continued structural injustice, but even in the face of atrocities like that of the massacre at Wiriyamu on 16 December 1972, when over 400 villagers were murdered by Portuguese soldiers. These Vatican

---

[6] A. Hastings, *Wiriyamu* (London, Search Press, 1974), 27; Appendix 1 (pp. 135–53) comprises the full texts of the Concordat, Missionary Agreement and Missionary Statute.

concordats are undoubtedly the most blatant instances of the use of Christianity to serve the interests of those in power.

However, if religion tends to be ideological, that is not the way it need be. The Catholic Church in Latin America provides an example of both ideological and utopian religion. Historically, the Catholic Church there came to be, generally speaking, part of the system, serving the interests of the land-owners, the military, the governing cliques and their foreign backers. It justified their power and position, and encouraged obedience, hard work and resignation on the part of the peasants. But in the last twenty years it became aware of the role it was playing, aware of whose interests it was promoting. A large part of it has refused to be so used any longer; it has consciously changed sides in a historic 'option for the poor' or commitment to the total welfare of the voiceless and the oppressed.

The division of Christianity into what I have called utopian and ideological forms is now the most significant division within Christianity. Divisions along the lines of denominations — Lutheran, Catholic, Reformed, Anglican — are, except in places like Northern Ireland where other factors keep them alive, no longer so important. In these main-line churches in the mid-1960s a revolution occurred in theology. All these churches, previously almost totally preoccupied with denominational orthodoxy, shifted the focus of their reflection outside the churches to society. Thus for the first time since the Reformation there arose the possibility of a truly interdenominational theology. The cause of this shift was the realization that traditional theology was wholly based on a naïve trust in the representational and objective value of ideas. The main-line churches belatedly accepted the devastating criticism that sociology had made of this naïve trust.[7] It is thus the social sciences that have revolutionized Christianity. Most Christians, when they think of the clash between science and religion, think of Darwin and the physical sciences and the nineteenth-century debates on evolution, after which Christians grudgingly conceded that the world was not created 6000 years ago as the Bible had previously been understood to teach. In fact, though, the impact of the physical sciences on Christianity was as nothing in comparison with the effect that the historical sciences — particularly in the form of what is called 'biblical criticism' — have had. But neither the

---

[7] A. Fierro, *The Militant Gospel: An Analysis of Contemporary Political Theologies* (London, SCM, 1977 [Spanish original, 1975]), 19.

physical nor the historical sciences have caused the revolution that the social sciences are presently effecting, and will continue to effect.[8]

It is not any particular conclusion of any of these sciences that has made the impact. It is the whole mentality that underlies these sciences, which we can call 'modernity'. To quote the Bergers:

> The issue here, quite simply, is the issue of modernity — but not modernity as an assemblage of techniques. After all, most traditionalist conservatives have made their peace with the telephone, the computer, and bypass surgery. The issue rather is in the area of modern consciousness, and specifically the experience of relativity — the awareness that all world views and value systems are contingent upon specific historical and social circumstances.[9]

Modernity, then, is defined as the awareness that all perceptions of the world or reality are not simply given. 'The world' is constructed by human perceptions, concerns and interests. 'Reality', therefore, differs from society to society and from age to age. This applies to Christianity, too. Within main-line Christianity, many tried to avoid the full implications of this by attempting something of a holding operation: by admitting the cultural and historical conditioning of the inessentials, but insisting that the essentials (usually termed 'revelation', understood as a hard core of trans-cultural, atemporal propositions or facts) were immune from the relativizing effects of cultural conditioning. But the attempt was unsuccessful.[10] Nothing human is immune, and revelation, whatever else it may be, is also a human reality. Since it is the social sciences that have rendered this conclusion inescapable, it is the social sciences (and especially the sociology of knowledge) that constitute the great bogey for all those who wish to reject modernity — not least the fundamentalist Christians.

Liberation theology, then, is nothing more than Christian reflection done from this attitude of modernity, or done with some sociological awareness.

---

[8] P. L. Berger, *A Rumour of Angels: Modern Society and the Rediscovery of the Supernatural* (Harmondsworth, Penguin, 1970), 46–7. But cf. O. Chadwick, *The Secularization of the European Mind in the Nineteenth Century* (Cambridge, Cambridge Univ. Press, 1975), 226.

[9] Berger and Berger, 'Our conservatism', 63. Peter Berger has written extensively on this modern experience of relativity and its consequences for religion. Besides the books cited in these footnotes, also relevant are his *An Invitation to Sociology: A Humanistic Perspective* (Harmondsworth, Penguin, 1966), and *The Sacred Canopy: Elements of a Sociological Theory of Religion* (New York, Doubleday, 1967).

[10] Berger, *A Rumour of Angels*, 55–7. The Catholic Church first officially admitted the historical conditioning of revelation in 1973 in *Mysterium Ecclesiae*, a conservative document of the Doctrinal Congregation reacting to Hans Küng's challenge to infallibility; see R. E. Brown, *Biblical Reflections on Crises Facing the Church* (London, Darton, Longman and Todd, 1975), 116–18.

87

It is not that these theologians set out to deny traditional Christian doctrines; it is just that they are aware that all traditional doctrines inevitably reflect the circumstances and cultures in which they were first articulated. Thus they realize that taking over doctrines formulated in previous ages is a much more complicated exercise than it was ever considered in the past. Nor is it that these Christians commit themselves to social reform as a substitute for personal morality or piety; it is just that their sociological awareness makes them far more alert to their inevitable social and political involvement and, therefore, far less given to exclusively personal morality and individualistic piety than Christians have been in the past. Nor do they deny the next world to focus entirely on this; they are simply aware that excessive focusing on the next world can often mask complicity in injustice in this world. Nor do they forget that Christian salvation involves deliverance from sin and guilt; they merely insist that, in the light of our present understanding, salvation can no longer be restricted to that. Christian salvation must be extended to include liberation from 'fate' (the idea that nothing can be done) and from oppression.

Nor do these liberation theologians advocate violence; they realize, however, that tremendous violence can be inflicted by oppressive systems, and they seek to reform such unjust structures. Where such reform is impossible in any peaceful way, many would say that the use of violence as a last resort cannot be excluded. Far from making them advocates of violence, however, this position makes them little different from proponents of the just war theory which has traditionally been embraced by a broad stream within Christianity. Nor is liberation theology just 'warmed over Marxism', as the *Wall Street Journal* described a 1967 papal encyclical.[11] Naturally, anyone familiar with the social sciences is aware of the contribution of Marx to social theory. Any scientist stands in a tradition, and a social scientist stands in a tradition formed by Marx and Durkheim and Weber and others. A social scientist will be continually drawing on the insights of the major figures in the tradition. Some will be more dependent on this major thinker, others on that. Some may find the contribution of Marx to the analysis of society particularly helpful, but this need involve no confusion of Marxism with Christianity. Ernesto Cardenal, a priest and Minister of Culture in Nicaragua's Sandinista Government stated his own position thus:

[11] R. McA. Brown, *Theology in a New Key: Responding to Liberation Themes* (Philadelphia, Westminister Press, 1978), 32.

There's no incompatibility between Christianity and Marxism. They aren't the same thing — they're different — but they're not incompatible. Christianity and the system called democracy aren't the same thing, but they're not incompatible. Again, Christianity and medical science, for example, aren't the same thing, but they're not incompatible. Marxism is a scientific method for studying society and changing it. What Christ did was to present us with the goals of social change, the goals of perfect humanity, which we are to co-create with him. These goals are a community of brothers and sisters, and love. But he did not tell us which scientific methods to use in order to arrive at the goal. Science has to tell us this — in our case, the social sciences. Some take one science, others another. But if anyone substitutes Marxism for Christianity, that person has made a mistake, just as if he or she were to take any other social science and substitute it for Christianity. Correctly understood, Marxism and Christianity are not incompatible.

This insistence that one can use insights originating from Marx as analytical tools, without in any way confusing Christianity and Marxism, is repeated by other liberation theologians, too.[12]

If liberation theology is Christian reflection done with some sociological awareness, it must be said that it is the complete lack of any sociological awareness that characterizes fundamentalists. (Of course, it is possible that some fundamentalists are fully aware of the role their Christianity plays, and propagate it precisely for its social, political and economic effects; any reader of Mark Twain, Sinclair Lewis, or even of *Time* and *Newsweek* between 1986 and 1988, would be well aware of the possibility. The possibility is even greater for the political and financial backers of the religious right. But the point of these pages is not to demonstrate the hypocrisy of fundamentalists, but to illustrate the social effects of their Christianity, irrespective of their motivation.) Their lack of sociological awareness explains their emphasis on exclusively personal motivation,

[12] For Cardenal's views, see T. Cabestrero, *Ministers of God, Ministers of the People: Testimonies of Faith from Nicaragua* (Maryknoll NY, Orbis, 1983 [Spanish original, 1982]), 31–2. Two of the most influential liberation theologians make the same point. Thus, Gustavo Gutiérrez: 'I have tried to reflect on the Christian experience of the poor. And for this, it's necessary to understand poverty and identify its causes. To do that, we must make use of all the instruments made available to us by human sciences. In social sciences, some notions come from Marxist analysis. But on the basis of that to want to make a synthesis of Christian faith and Marxism is impossible — there is a yawning gap. Moreover such a synthesis would be about as absurd as a synthesis between Christian faith and Einsteinian physics', interview with *Le Monde* (5 Feb. 1985), reprinted in the *Guardian Weekly* (17 Feb. 1985), 12; and Leonardo Boff: 'Our theology has always meant to utilise Marxism as a means, an intellectual tool, an instrument of social analysis. This is Marxism's epistemological status: it's the theology, not the Marxism, that is in the position of the theoretical objective. It's true, Marxism is dangerous, but it seems no less useful for grasping the social reality, especially concerning poverty and its elimination', quoted in the *Guardian Weekly* (26 Aug. 1984), 12.

personal sin, private morality; it explains their exclusive reliance on prayer and the miraculous, and the example of one's personal life to effect change; it explains their emphasis on the next world, and the prominence given to obedience. It also explains the claim of many (though not all, by any means) that religion and politics do not mix. As McAfee Brown has said, religion and politics are inevitably mixed; the only question is, what is the nature of the mix — what kind of religion, issuing in what kind of politics?[13]

But fundamentalism lacks not only sociological awareness, it lacks historical awareness, too. Fundamentalists put great stress on the depravity of the world and humankind, fathering their understanding of 'original sin' on the Bible, without realizing that it comes from Augustine of Hippo (AD 354–430).[14] Similarly, they read back their Trinitarian orthodoxy into the Bible without realizing that it comes from Athanasius (AD 296–373).[15] The only understanding of Christ's death that they allow to be Christian is the theory of substitutionary penal atonement (that is, that Christ died in man's place to appease an angry God) unaware that the theory comes from Anselm of Canterbury (AD 1033–1109) and that it is inconceivable outside the culture of the high Middle Ages in which he lived.[16] They use the Bible simplistically, taking texts to be immediately relevant, paying little attention to the original context. Above all, they make biblical inerrancy pivotal, without realizing that the whole notion is a seventeenth-century invention or even, in the way many formulate it, a nineteenth-century one.[17] But we can go even further: if fundamentalism is untouched by sociological or historical awareness, it is also this sector of Christianity that is concerned to defend 'scientifically' the biblical accounts of the Creation ('creation science', they call it) and of the Flood, which indicates that they have difficulty with the physical sciences as well. The main-line churches have accepted the physical, historical and social sciences, and the mentality underlying them. So, again, it is obvious that the point of division between these two kinds of Christianity is not at the level of any particular doctrine: it is at the far more basic level of accepting the modern world. This is the

[13] Brown, 'Listen, Jerry Falwell!', 360.
[14] P. Brown, *Augustine of Hippo* (London, Faber, 1967), 391–7.
[15] Barr, *Fundamentalism*, 16.
[16] J. Pelikan, *Jesus through the Centuries: His Place in the History of Culture* (New Haven, Yale Univ. Press, 1985), 107–8. See also G. Aulén, *Christus Victor: An Historical Study of the Three Main Types of the Idea of the Atonement* (New York, Macmillan, 1969 [German original, 1930]).
[17] Barr, *Fundamentalism*, 175; Barr, 'The problem of fundamentalism today', 88.

logic behind the fundamentalists' charge that the main-line churches have sold out to 'modernity', or succumbed to 'the modern world'. They mean this as a criticism. The main-line churches reply that this is the only way a modern person can be a Christian.

One key point should be obvious: the novelty of liberation theology. Liberation theology *is* new. It must be, for its approach depends on insights provided by the social sciences. It could not have existed before they made their contribution. It is anachronistic to think that it did or should have. Mention has been made above of the White Fathers' decision to leave Mozambique rather than appear to collaborate with the bishops in Portuguese oppression. Their criticism was that the bishops were trying 'to consolidate and perpetuate an anachronism'. Exactly. Whatever may have been the rights and wrongs of Catholic mission policy in the past, the policy is indefensible in the light of present understanding. From a new standpoint, a reappraisal is necessary. Liberation theology itself sometimes de-emphasizes its real element of novelty, most often by implying that the Prophet Amos or the Apostle Paul really said all this long ago. Amos or Paul may have said things which are in harmony with aspects of contemporary thinking, but they had no knowledge of modern sociology. It does them no service to claim that they did.

Of course, one can readily understand why liberation theologians tend to present Amos or Paul as early liberation theologians, because Christianity has always understood itself and presented itself as something unchanging, as a 'faith once and for all delivered to the saints' (Jude 3). 'Novelty' has traditionally been a very dirty word in Christianity. In Catholicism, the strand of Christianity where the anti-novelty attitude was most marked in recent centuries, it was even said that someone could spend the first half of his life discovering something new, and the second half trying to show that it was not new at all.[18] Before the rise of the historical sciences it was perhaps natural to think that way, but after the rise of historical consciousness it is obvious that this was never the case. Christianity has been continually changing as the societies in which Christians lived changed. Sociological consciousness goes further and shows why this could never have been the case, why Christianity must have changed. Nothing human is transcultural, remaining unchanging if the society in which it is embodied changes.

[18] T. M. Schoof, *A Survey of Catholic Theology 1800–1970* (New York, Paulist Newman Press, 1970), 158.

Christianity has not remained unchanging; it cannot have remained unchanging; it does not have to remain unchanged. Whereas in the past Christian thinkers would have always stressed (because it was all they saw) the continuity between different expressions of Christianity, now many can see the real discontinuity between them. On any reckoning, Augustine of Hippo is one of the greatest figures in Christian history, but our world is so different from his that modern Christianity cannot be merely a reformulation of his. As one Christian writer puts it, 'Partly [Augustine] excites and confirms my deepest convictions; partly he arouses such disgust that I do not wish to share a faith such as his'.[19] Elsewhere, the same writer graphically stresses this genuine discontinuity in Christian history by stating that a room containing Augustine, Dunstan, Becket, Cranmer, Laud, Howley, Tait and Runcie — all of them Archbishops of Canterbury — 'would soon be a babble of mutual incomprehension'.[20] Of course, this awareness of discontinuities does not necessarily mean that there are no constants persisting through social changes. As the Bergers write, the experience of relativity

does not imply that there is no such thing as truth ... The experience of relativity, however, makes it difficult to hold beliefs in the taken-for-granted, untroubled way that has always been characteristic of tradition. The individual who has passed through the experience may hold very firm beliefs, but he will be conscious of the fact that he has chosen them. The traditionalist holds his beliefs as givens.[21]

One may still talk about constants, but not in the simplistic way people used to. So, too, within Christianity. Of course, there are continuities between traditional theology and the modern expressions we have called liberation theology, but there are very real discontinuities as well. There is genuine novelty. But this is nothing to be surprised about. One can now see that there have always been real discontinuities between successive expressions of Christianity.[22]

This point is worth labouring, because fundamentalists insist that,

---

[19] J. L. Houlden, *Patterns of Faith: A Study in the Relationship between the New Testament and Christian Doctrine* (London, SCM, 1977), 79.

[20] J. L. Houlden, *Connections* (London, SCM, 1986), 115.

[21] Berger and Berger, 'Our conservatism', 63. They write further on (ibid., 65): 'Traditionalists of all varieties keep on saying that there are absolute values. We do not really care to dispute this. Our problem is that we are not quite sure what these values are.'

[22] See N. Lash, *Change in Focus: A Study of Doctrinal Change and Continuity* (London, Sheed and Ward, 1973); and S. Sykes, *The Identity of Christianity* (London, SPCK, 1984). For the continuities and discontinuities between liberation theology and traditional Christianity, see Brown, *Theology in a New Key*, 19–74.

although the main-line churches have sold out to the modern world, they are the true Christians who preserve the 'old-time religion'. This claim to the ancient pristine form of Christianity is false, for two reasons.

The first reason has just been given. Christianity, whatever else it may be, is a social reality and thus cannot remain unaltered when society changes. When any kind of revolution takes place (and the advent of 'modernity' is an enormous revolution), it is one thing to live before the revolution, and quite another thing to turn one's back on it and act as if it had never occurred, after the revolution has taken place. It is only in a very artificial sense that a Christian today can claim to hold exactly the same beliefs as Augustine, Aquinas or Luther. As Alan Richardson writes:

The position of a man who insists after the Copernican revolution that the sun goes round the earth is not really the same position as that of the pre-Copernican astronomers. He has in fact taken up an attitude to evidence which the pre-Copernicans had not been able to consider, and which would in all reasonable probability have caused them to modify their Ptolemaic views, if they had had access to it. His attitude to the authority of Ptolemy is quite different from theirs; for them Ptolemy was the only known standard of truth, and accepting Ptolemy did not involve rejecting Copernicus.[23]

Secondly, far from being traditional or New Testament Christianity, fundamentalism is a very modern phenomenon. Fundamentalism is essentially a reaction against 'modern' Christianity. As we have observed, its central idea of biblical inerrancy is not the traditional Christian attitude to the Bible at all, but is something quite new, something thought up in reaction to questions 'modern' Christians were putting to the Bible. The fundamentalists' notion of biblical inerrancy is inconceivable without modernity. In other areas, too, the modern origins of fundamentalism are evident. The idea of truth for fundamentalists is the 'plain truth' of the eighteenth-century Enlightenment. In interpreting the Bible, they are interested in the question whether the event under consideration took place materially or physically. This is the kind of truth that matters. Questions of significance — religious significance — can be asked, if at all, only after this has been agreed. Barr writes:

Non-conservative theology begins much more with the question about signifi-

[23] A. Richardson, 'The rise of modern biblical scholarship and recent discussion of the authority of the Bible', in S. L. Grenslade (ed.), *Cambridge History of the Bible: III* (Cambridge, Cambridge Univ. Press, 1963), 310.

cance: what does it mean that this is narrated in this form? It is a reasonable comment, therefore, to say that the fundamentalist conception of truth is dominated by a materialistic view, derived from a scientific age. This stress on the accuracy of the Bible in its material–physical reporting separates modern fundamentalism entirely from that older theology, such as the theology of Luther and Calvin, which it ill-informedly claims as its own forebear.[24]

Both Barr and Marsden insist that the theological method of fundamentalists was formed on the analogy of natural science, and natural science as seen in a traditional Newtonian mould.[25] This factor probably explains fundamentalism's attraction for those with a modern technical education.[26] At a recent conference on religion there was even talk of the 'engineering mentality' of fundamentalists.[27] They see religion as involving 'hard facts' and proper techniques that are fairly straightforward but do demand competence in their application. Thus, they tend to view religion somewhat as the average person and the technician tend to view science. It is not accidental that both Jerry Falwell and Francis Schaeffer studied engineering at college.[28] Fitzgerald, in her very critical discussion of education at Falwell's Liberty University ('It is simply the process of learning, or teaching, the right answers') supports this:

At the Liberty Baptist Schools, students are protected both from information and from most logical processes. There is no formal ban on logic, but since analytical reasoning might lead to scepticism, and scepticism to the questioning of biblical truth, it is simply not encouraged except in disciplines like engineering, where it could be expected to yield a single correct answer. (Not coincidentally, some of the brightest people I met at Thomas Road, including Falwell himself, had studied engineering.) In anything resembling human affairs, the intellectual discipline consists of moving word sticks and fact sticks from one pile to another with the minimum coefficient of friction.[29]

[24] Barr, *Fundamentalism*, 93. On the whole question of the novelty of fundamentalism, see ibid., 90–110, 270–96, 315.

[25] Ibid., 93; Marsden, *Fundamentalism and American Culture*, 55–62 (this is referred to in Shepard, ' "Fundamentalism": Christian and Islamic', 365). Marsden makes the same point stressing fundamentalism's links with 'Scottish Common Sense Philosophy', *Fundamentalism and American Culture*, 110–12.

[26] Barr, *Fundamentalism*, 93, 272–5.

[27] Conference of the International Association for the History of Religion, Sydney, Australia, 22 Aug. 1985, during discussion after N. C. Nielson's paper entitled 'Fundamentalism as a Crosscultural Phenomenon'.

[28] Shepard, ' "Fundamentalism": Christian and Islamic', 377 n.51. Francis Schaeffer was the founder of L'Abri Fellowship, Huemoz, Switzerland.

[29] Fitzgerald, *Cities on a Hill*, 159; see also 154, 158–60, 198–200. Shepard notes that in Muslim fundamentalism there is the same prominence of engineers and those with similar technical training, ' "Fundamentalism": Christian and Islamic', 377 n.51.

It cannot be too often repeated that the kind of 'traditional religion' to which return is urged is nearly always a figment of a very unhistorical imagination. The 'eternal, unchanging Christianity', on investigation, turns out to be a nineteenth-century construct. Far from being Christianity before modernity emerged, it is something worked out in opposition to modernity which had already emerged.[30]

The Bergers state that if the first quality of modernity is the awareness of the relativity of every human product, the second is a pragmatic 'tinkering'.[31] This has its equivalent in modern theology, too, in 'praxis' or concern for action. This second aspect flows from the first. Once one is aware of the socially constructed nature of our world, aware of the fact that knowledge or reality or society is not simply dropped from heaven as a given, but is a product of human perceptions and interests, it becomes impossible to view the world as something immutable, something naturally thus. From this arises the realization that it is possible to improve the world; to make social structures less unjust is a real option. Another realization arises, too: to acquiesce in the present state of things is no less a conscious choice.

All the above may give the impression that liberation theology is an academic exercise. It can be: there are learned books which discuss social theory, analyse society in terms of academic models, and take issue with the ideas of other scholars. But this kind of reflection is not primarily that. It is essentially a popular thing, done by ordinary people reflecting on their own experience, people who have read nothing of Marx and who would perhaps understand little if they tried. People with little formal education can articulate their experience, analyse their situation, recognize structures, make connections, see imperfections and propose alternatives. And those among them who are Christians can do all this in the light of Christianity. Ernesto Cardenal's four-volume *The Gospel in Solentiname*, for example, is exactly this — peasants of a Nicaraguan fishing village reflecting on the Gospel each Sunday in the light of their experience, or, as many would prefer to put it, reflecting on their own experience in the light of the Gospel.[32] Thus, this kind of Christianity is available to all.

Why this form of Christianity should have taken root in Latin America

---

[30] Exactly the same process was at work within official Catholicism of the last hundred years: see B. McSweeney, *Roman Catholicism: The Search for Relevance* (Oxford, Blackwell, 1980).

[31] Berger and Berger, 'Our conservatism', 63.

[32] E. Cardenal, *The Gospel in Solentiname* (Maryknoll NY, Orbis, 4 vols., 1976–82).

and not Africa is an interesting question. Various suggestions have been advanced. It is sometimes said that in Latin America the colonial era ended centuries ago, whereas in Africa decolonization began only recently. Thus, in Africa, colonialism could be viewed as the crucial issue, something which could not be argued in Latin America. Somewhat paradoxically, others say that in Latin America the overwhelming economic involvement of the USA (that is, American neo-colonialism) raises the question of economic exploitation in a way it is not raised in Africa. Others claim that in Africa the presence of Europeans and the dominance of their culture has focused attention on the issue of culture rather than on economic structures. Others, again paradoxically, explain the African focus on cultural rather than economic issues from the fact that in Africa local cultures still provide human support, whereas Latin America has seen its indigenous cultures far more thoroughly destroyed. Another complicating factor in Africa is that of race, which militates against a single issue (namely, economic) analysis which is possible in Latin America. A difference in the scale of poverty has also been suggested: Africa (it is said), except after natural disasters, has not experienced the extremes of poverty which are the norm in the *barrios* and *favelas* in Latin America. Some argue that the dispossession of the many and the corresponding enrichment of the few have not been so great or so glaringly obvious in Africa: no African country has the equivalent of El Salvador's fourteen families, for example, or a situation like that in Paraguay where 1 per cent of the population owns 80 per cent of the land.

Others point to the different nature of the Church on the two continents. Latin America is almost monolithically Catholic, which has permitted a more uniform response than is possible in Africa, where Christianity is far more heterogeneous. And the hierarchical structure of the Catholic Church, particularly now with Bishops' Conferences organized for entire regions and even continents, facilitates a more concerted response than is possible in denominations whose churches are more autonomous. Some claim that Catholicism in Latin America has come to be far less institutionalized: in places, it exists as base communities and little else. In Africa, by contrast, several churches are enormously institutionalized: the Catholics in Zaïre, for example, run an enterprise almost parallel to the state. Successfully running schools, hospitals, training centres and workshops requires considerable effort and attention, which in Latin America can be devoted to structural analysis. There may be some truth in all these suggestions.

Is the fact that liberation theology took root in a Catholic environment significant? We have called any such religion 'utopian'. The Bergers have claimed that of all the main streams of Christianity (Orthodoxy, Catholicism, Lutheranism, Anglicanism, the Reformed tradition) Lutheranism is the 'most anti-utopian' because of its insistence that salvation comes by faith, not by any human effort, and because its doctrine of the Two Kingdoms, one of grace and one of law, presents this world as no place to expect perfection.[33] Is the converse true? Is Catholicism's alleged emphasis on works or effort or activity part of the reason for liberation theology's stress on programmatic reform? Probably not, for within Catholicism the works were traditionally calculated to earn rewards in the next life, not to influence this. And also, even though liberation theology took root in Latin America, its less immediate origins were in the theology faculties of Germany, where Lutheranism is part of the air that is breathed. Probably, that liberation theology took root within Catholicism is a historical and geographical accident. Latin America is Catholic because the Spanish and Portuguese colonists made it difficult for other denominations to gain a foothold. It was the indescribable poverty and the appalling injustice of Latin America that provided the context for the development of liberation theology. It may have arisen in a Catholic environment, but all the main-line churches have absorbed it.

Paradoxically, for something that arose in the overwhelmingly Catholic countries of Latin America, liberation theology has encountered considerable resistance from the Vatican. This opposition, however, is to be explained not so much in terms of the merits or demerits of liberation theology, as by recent Catholic history and by the personality and background of the present Pope. The last 150 years saw a massive centralization within the Catholic Church, with all power coming to be vested in Rome. This process began to be reversed by the Second Vatican Council (1962–5), which advocated a form of power-sharing ('collegiality') and initiated a process of devolution to local churches. That reversal, however, ended with the election of John Paul II in October 1978. He came to the papacy with great gifts, but also

filled with the preoccupations of the Polish Church's struggle with Communism. He had been through all the sessions of the [Second Vatican] Council as a fairly young

---

[33] Berger and Berger, 'Our conservatism', 66.

man, but would not appear to have imbibed much of its deeper re-orientations and the sort of experience from which they derived in Western Europe, Latin America and the southern hemisphere generally.[34]

More importantly, he is a centralist. Far from encouraging devolution to local churches, he wants all power to be gathered up in Rome again. In the 1980s, especially through extensive world tours, 'papal monarchy and the personality cult of the Pope were back with a force, an attractiveness, an omni-presence never known before'.[35] It is this centralism more than fear of Marxism that explains Rome's opposition to liberation theology. For liberation theology is essentially theology from the underside, or from the grass roots. Liberation theology came from Latin America, not from Rome, and even in Latin America it came from the clergy and lay people of the base communities, not from the hierarchy. This is a complete reversal of the procedures accepted within Catholicism in the last 150 years. The desire to see those older procedures re-established explains, for example, why on his 1987 visit to the US church, the Pope made no reference to the remarkable contribution of the US Catholic Bishops with their pastoral letters on the nuclear issue (1983) and the economy (1986). To give favourable notice to those letters would have conferred papal legitimacy on the teaching function of national conferences of bishops, as distinct from Rome.[36]

Rome's opposition to liberation theology has been increased because liberation theology analyses not only the structures of the State, but also those within the Church. The Brazilian Franciscan, Leonardo Boff, analyses these Catholic structures in *Church, Charisma, Power*, and is decidedly critical of the monarchic and pyramidal hierarchy of the Church, and the way these structures have been used, particularly over the last 150 years.[37]

It is these internal Catholic reasons — these different understandings of the nature of the Church and its teaching authority — that are the principal reasons for Rome's opposition to liberation theology. On 3 September 1984, the Congregation for the Doctrine of the Faith, headed by Cardinal Ratzinger, issued its *Instructions on Some Aspects of the Theology of Liberation*, which was very negative in tone, dwelling on the dangers of

[34] A. Hastings, *A History of English Christianity 1920–85* (London, Collins, 1986), 642.
[35] Ibid., 643.
[36] R. McBrien, 'Varieties of dissent', *Tablet* (10 Oct. 1987), 1081.
[37] L. Boff, *Church, Charisma, Power: Liberation Theology and the Institutional Church* (New York, Crossroad, 1985).

polluting Catholicism with foreign concepts taken from Marxism. Only twenty months later, however, on 5 April 1986, the same Congregation issued another document on *Christian Freedom and Liberation*, which, although withdrawing none of its warnings about Marxism, took a very different line. It was still ambiguous enough to elicit completely contradictory headlines from two of the world's major newspapers. *The Times* of London, on its front page, summed up the document thus: 'The Vatican has effectively removed armed struggle as a means by which Roman Catholics may oppose tyranny';[38] the *New York Times'* front-page headline read, 'Vatican Backs Struggle by Poor to End Injustice'.[39] Most, surely correctly, understood the document in this second way. The document proclaimed that it was 'perfectly legitimate that those who suffer oppression on the part of the wealthy or politically powerful should take action', and made it clear that 'armed struggle' was considered permissible as a 'last resort to put an end to an obvious and prolonged tyranny which is gravely damaging the fundamental rights of individuals and the common good'. It also affirmed that 'the right to private property . . . is subordinated to the higher principle which states that goods are meant for all'.[40]

This document undoubtedly represents a new position on the part of the Vatican. Gustavo Gutiérrez of Peru was elated, taking this as final vindication of the liberation theology he had helped to pioneer. 'This marks the end of an era', he said. 'The debate [between the Vatican and liberation theology] is closed'.[41] This second document is probably best seen as a grudging recognition by Rome that it was powerless to counter the popular groundswell in favour of liberation theology.[42]

I have been using the expression 'liberation theology' in a general sense or as an umbrella term for any kind of 'utopian' Christianity, any Christianity that refuses to focus exclusively on privatized morality and individual sanctification, but also looks at the social structures within which Christians operate, aware that men and women have created those structures and are, therefore, responsible for the evil and injustice inflicted by them. It is this approach that liberation theologians have in common, not specific

---

[38] *The Times* (7 Apr. 1986), 1.
[39] *New York Times* (6 Apr. 1986), 1.
[40] Cited in ibid., 14.
[41] See *Newsweek* (14 Apr. 1986), 44.
[42] O'Brien, 'God and man in Nicaragua', 65–6.

conclusions or programmes. In Latin America, the structures tend to be considered in specifically economic terms. As Baum has argued, in Latin America economic oppression is so basic, so determinative of every facet of life, that an analysis from a narrowly economic angle may commit no serious distortion. But in many other countries, an analysis restricted to purely economic categories would not do justice to the complexity of the situation.[43] So the liberation theology produced in Latin America cannot be transferred immediately to other places. The approach can, however. In the West, considerable attention has been given to structures as they affect women; thus has developed feminist theology. In North America, attention has been given to structures which oppress subordinated cultures; thus has developed Black theology. Even within a particular area, there may be considerable differences — the lot of women in the USA, for example, is very different from their lot in Africa. Thus, liberation theology is not only new, as has been argued above, it is also contextual, or takes different forms in different circumstances. Obviously, those who think in terms of eternal truths, unchanging human nature, reality as a given, will be less ready to see this pluralism as a virtue, and will be less happy that Christianity should be acculturated differently in various places, and in forms different from those of the past. To regard contextualization as a virtue obviously presupposes the acceptance of relativity which, as we have seen, is the key factor in 'modernity'.

So, liberation theology is not a single package. It is an approach. Of those who adopt this approach, some will be more radical, others less so. The approach will be modified as the debate continues. What were originally considered less central elements may become more important as time goes on. Conversely, some emphases may come to be seen as overdone. For example, Gutiérrez's *A Theology of Liberation*, one of the most important academic works in this field, makes a good deal of the economic theory of dependency. That theory has come to be eclipsed somewhat, so, although the book remains a classic, some of its arguments would no longer be put forward in exactly that way.[44] Some exponents of this approach twist biblical materials, making, for example, Israel's exodus from Egypt a pattern of political liberation, or making Jesus out to be a proto Che Guevara. Certainly, criticism can be made of every liberation theologian. Like every

[43] Baum, *Religion and Alienation*, 216–20.
[44] G. Gutiérrez, *A Theology of Liberation* (Maryknoll NY, Orbis, 1973 [Spanish original, 1971]).

current of human thinking, it undoubtedly has its lunatic fringe. But this does not prove that the whole enterprise is wrong-headed: it merely shows that liberation theology is no different from any other field of human endeavour.

This sociological awareness has revolutionized the main-line Christian denominations in the last twenty years. The advance of this kind of Christianity is, as we have seen, considered a real threat to certain vested interests which have mobilized to discredit it. At the same time, fundamentalist Christianity has also spread, sometimes dramatically, particularly in places like Latin America and Africa. This phenomenon is sometimes linked with the rise of Muslim fundamentalism, which has taken power in Iran and considerably increased its influence in Africa. Is it helpful to see Christian fundamentalism as a movement parallel to Islamic fundamentalism? Is a comparison between them fruitful? Shepard has addressed precisely this question, and some of his conclusions are relevant here.[45]

He begins his discussion with two significant differences between the Christian and Islamic movements. First, the most important item in the definition of Christian fundamentalism, the inerrancy of the Bible, is entirely irrelevant in the Muslim case, since virtually all Muslims, including secularists, consider the Qur'an inerrant. Secondly, whereas Protestant fundamentalism has come to be very nationalist ('American' primarily, but also 'South African'), Muslim fundamentalism consciously rejects nationalism as a foreign ideology designed, among other things, to divide the Muslim community.

There are, however, numerous similarities, of varying degrees of significance. Both Christian and Muslim fundamentalism share an 'oppositional stance'; both are consciously opposed to 'modernity'.[46] Both have a certain minority consciousness, holding that 'true believers' are relatively few in number; paradoxically, this can be combined with a certain triumphalism about their achievements and influence. Both claim to be authentic expressions of their respective traditions; they claim to be the 'true Christians' or 'true Muslims'. Both tend to stress those elements that are most distinctive of the religious traditions of which they are a part — in the

---

[45] The following points are all taken from Shepard, ' "Fundamentalism": Christian and Islamic', 359–66.

[46] Fitzgerald works this out well in Falwell's case: Falwell secures his own authority by maintaining this tension between his followers and the world; Falwell *needs* enemies; see Fitzgerald, *Cities on a Hill*, 166–8. Barr, too, argues that opposition is of the essence of fundamentalism, *Fundamentalism*, 17.

Christian case, the Bible, original sin, the deity of Christ, the atonement; in the Muslim case, the Qur'an and Sunna, and Muslim social and political ideals. By contrast, the modern movements they are opposing have tended to give far greater prominence to things that are common to all major religions, like the ethical values of love and justice. Both fundamentalisms tend to see everything in black-and-white terms. Both are characterized by a reluctance to interpret; where possible, both want to keep to the 'plain sense' of the text. (For Christian fundamentalists, however, this consideration is subordinate to the absolute inerrancy of the Bible: where possible, they will hold to a common-sense reading, but where it is necessary to preserve the Bible's inerrancy, they will resort to all kinds of non-literal interpretations. Thus it is incorrect to consider 'literalness' as the key characteristic of fundamentalist use of the Bible.)[47] Both are characterized by a certain ecumenical tendency, stemming from the sense that when under threat true believers should forget secondary differences; of course, this ecumenical tendency has nothing to do with the ecumenical movement of mainstream Christianity, which fundamentalists regard with disdain. Both consciously measure modern developments by standards which they claim are drawn from the past, and both would like to go back to a golden era. For Muslims, this is probably the period just before the onslaught of Western imperialism, whereas, for Christians, this period would be the New Testament times as they imagine them, and the early nineteenth century when American fundamentalists seem to think the idea of a Christian society was most closely realized.[48]

Both are characterized by their activism — they want to shape, form, or at least influence, governments. In this, both reject the quietist tendencies in their traditions. Both have a fairly 'moralistic', even 'puritanical', view of personal ethics, including a fairly strong Weberian work ethic, and a strong sense that the well-being of society is highly dependent on personal morality. Both, though effectively reacting against the modern world, have quite enthusiastically accepted some of what modernity has to offer; Christian fundamentalism, for example, has made far more use of the electronic mass media than main-line Christianity, and smuggled cassettes of Ayatollah Khomeini's talks were a key element in the Iranian revolution. Both would claim to function at both a popular and a more intellectual level;

---

[47] Barr, *Fundamentalism*, 40–55.
[48] Note that Fitzgerald places Falwell's golden age in the 1930s, *Cities on a Hill*, 181.

both may seem rather 'rabble-rousing' in their approach, but they would insist that they belong to an intellectual tradition.[49] Both would claim to find their main authority in a written scripture rather than in an authoritarian clergy and priesthood, or in ritual and sacrament, or in a distinctive subjective spiritual experience.

In the light of the similarities, Shepard concludes that Christian and Islamic fundamentalism have enough in common to justify a common label, at least for comparative purposes. But the word's emotive overtones, its pejorative connotations, and its specifically Western cultural origins make 'fundamentalism' unable to do justice to the subtleties of the Islamic phenomenon, for which he prefers a term like 'Islamic radicalism'. Shepard makes a good case for his position. However, my purpose in outlining his comparison is to adduce his support for a key point in these pages, that is, the essential novelty of fundamentalism. Shepard shows that both fundamentalisms are essentially reactions against modernity. Both are reacting against a modernity which stresses reason over 'revelation' as the source of knowledge, de-emphasizes the supernaturalistic, and tends to be both relativistic and universalistic in ethics. In opposition to this modernity, both fundamentalisms claim authenticity in tradition, both hark back to the past, both advocate 'eternally valid' truths, a supernaturalistic world view, and absolutism in ethics.[50]

Shepard's comparison suggests a very plausible reason why fundamentalism should be spreading in Zimbabwe. Such movements seem to grow in places where social change is perceived as especially threatening. Shepard notes that the 'social and psychological alienation resulting from certain aspects of modernity seems to be an important motivating factor in both cases'. He notes that Muslim fundamentalism is an almost exclusively urban phenomenon, 'because it is in the urban areas where the alien pressures to which it is reacting have been mainly felt'.[51] Marsden had already drawn attention to the origins of fundamentalism in the United States in the 1920s, proposing that a major factor in its emergence was the shocked realization that what had, fifty years earlier, been a predominant cultural consensus had disappeared. Marsden thus suggests that

---

[49] Barr, *Fundamentalism*, thoroughly explodes these intellectual pretensions.
[50] The supernatural (for example, God, heaven, prayer) is not played down in main-line Christianity, merely the supernaturalistic (for example, special revelations, special divine interventions).
[51] Shepard, ' "Fundamentalism": Christian and Islamic', 366.

103

fundamentalism is related to an Anglo-Saxon analogue to the immigrant experience.[52] In South Africa, the tremendously threatening socio-political scene helps explain the growth in the fundamentalist churches. A study of these churches produced by the Centre for Applied Social Sciences at the University of Natal captures this in its title: *Faith for the Fearful?*[53] This is the argument the sociologist Mary de Haas makes in her investigation of why Whites in South Africa are joining these churches. She suggests that:

these movements offer a home to people who have become painfully aware that their very future is at stake. In other words, by a process of 'elective affinity' in the Weberian sense, widely different groups of people have found solace, in different ways, in the face of a situation which is perceived as threatening. There is still hope of redemption from a future which appears bleak and fraught with uncertainty . . . These Reborn movements, in offering assurance of worldly success as well as spiritual salvation, minimize the threat posed by possible future changes in the status quo, and divert attention from the uncomfortable realities of contemporary South Africa, realities which the mainline churches, conscious of their prophetic ministry, are attempting to bring to the attention of their flocks.[54]

De Haas is expressly talking about Whites, but the situation is no less threatening for many Blacks. And the situation in Zimbabwe can appear just as threatening. To point this out is not to belittle the very real fears of people in these circumstances, or to manifest intellectual or psychological superiority over those who feel them. However, it is doubtful whether, in the long run, fundamentalism does anything to meet these fears. It is suggested here that the main-line churches have adopted the more constructive course: that of facing the uncomfortable realities, even admitting some responsibility for them, and working for change in the structures that cause them.

There are other reasons, too, for the spread of these churches in the last few

---

[52] Marsden, *Fundamentalism and American Culture*, 205.

[53] See Morran and Schlemmer, *Faith for the Fearful?*, esp. 21–45, where they discuss various theoretical approaches — social disorganization, deprivation, authoritarian personality, meaning and belonging theories — to account for this phenomenon. See also Valderrey, 'Sects in Central America', 5, 22–5; Baum, *Religion and Alienation*, 152; Secretariat for Promoting Christian Unity, *Report on Sects*.

[54] De Haas, 'Is millenarianism alive and well in White South Africa?', 40–1. For a historical survey of revivalist movements that have arisen in times of change, see R. Knox, *Enthusiasm: A Chapter in the History of Religion* (Oxford, Oxford Univ. Press, 1962), and N. Cohn, *The Pursuit of the Millennium: Revolutionary Millenarians and Mystical Anarchists of the Middle Ages* (London, Paladin, 1970 [original, 1957]). Fitzgerald sheds a good deal of light on current American revivalism by comparing it to the period of America's Second Great Awakening, using the anthropological theories of A. F. C. Wallace ('revitalization movements') and Victor Turner ('liminal transitions'); see Fitzgerald, *Cities on a Hill*, 383–414.

years. One is, undoubtedly, their financial resources. Most of them are derived from, or linked to, or in harmony with, North American churches. In this way they have access to substantial funds there. Fund-raising trips to the United States are a regular occurrence for many of these pastors. This in itself is significant. Most of the American churches from which the funds come subscribe to the whole politico-religious agenda of the religious right. Presumably, they give the money for the furtherance of that agenda. Presumably, also, Zimbabwean pastors have to be in sympathy with that agenda to qualify for the money. As mentioned above, this was the case with Shekinah Ministries. The funding of these churches is something the ZCC has drawn attention to.[55]

Another reason for the spread of this fundamentalist Christianity is personnel. The main-line Protestant churches have decreased their missionary effort in Africa. This withdrawal has occurred not just because there are fewer missionaries volunteering. The withdrawal is a result of the conscious decision of the main-line churches (expressed, for example, at the Lusaka meeting of the All-Africa Conference of Churches in 1974) that local churches must provide their own leaders if they are to be truly local churches, with a kind of Christianity appropriate to themselves, rather than facsimiles of their European or American models. However, since the mid-1960s, the number of missionaries on the continent has remained fairly constant. The departing main-line missionaries have been replaced by others, particularly from the southern United States.[56]

Also relevant is the use made of these considerable human and financial resources. There is a clear distinction here between the main-line and the pentecostal–fundamentalist churches. The human and financial resources of the main-line churches have in recent years become heavily committed to development — consider in Zimbabwe, for example, the massive Lutheran World Federation commitment to development projects, or the Catholic involvement through its development agency CADEC. By contrast, the efforts of the pentecostal–fundamentalist churches are heavily weighted towards Christian evangelization and, when they go beyond that, towards relief work. Their evangelization takes various forms: 'services to local churches', 'leadership training' for local pastors, 'church planting'.

[55] *Sunday Mail* (17 Nov. 1985), 1.
[56] A. Hastings, *A History of African Christianity, 1950–1975* (Cambridge, Cambridge Univ. Press, 1979), 224–8.

They would all insist that they are developing or planting not any denomination in particular but 'Christianity' pure and simple. But, as I have remarked more than once above, this is false. The type of Christianity they are promoting, to which they rather arrogantly restrict the word 'Christian', is a particular form of Christianity developed in the southern states of America. There is nothing African, or local, or contextual, about this Christianity. As Huntington writes, 'The most striking characteristic of Central American Protestantism is that it is the product of foreign — primarily North American — evangelical mission activity. Its theology was conceived, financed, and packaged in Texas, Missouri, California and the Bible Belt, then translated directly into Spanish'.[57] If we substitute local languages for Spanish, we have the same situation in Southern Africa.

That the pentecostal–fundamentalist churches are involved in relief, while the main-line churches are committed to development, supports the basic argument of these pages. The rationale behind relief work is different from that behind development. Relief work is motivated by benevolence or charity, and it is a response to particular suffering. Development is something more. It is motivated not by benevolence but by concerns of social justice, and is a response to a situation in which people are considered to be prevented from leading full lives. Development aims at transforming the socio-economic situation in which people find themselves. Thus, development involves some social analysis, asking questions like, 'Who created the structures of this society? Who maintains them? Who benefits from them? And how disproportionate is this benefit?' Development also involves a commitment to socio-political change in the direction of greater equality, of greater power to the poor; to long-term changes which go well beyond relieving some specific suffering. It is obvious, therefore, why some would like Christians to restrict themselves to relief work, why they say that relief (charity) is the Christian activity, and that anything beyond is unwarranted interference in politics. The point is well made by the oft-quoted words of Helder Camara: 'When I give bread to the poor they call me a saint. When I ask why the poor have no bread they call me a communist'.[58]

---

[57] Huntington, 'The prophet motive', 3.

[58] Other factors, too, can combine to keep the pentecostal–fundamentalist churches out of development. Some hold that the world is irredeemable, thoroughly depraved and under Satan; the strongly dispensationalist hold that the world is passing away anyway; adherents to the gospel of prosperity tend to hold that the poor are not saved, for if they were saved they would be rich too.

One other aspect of this pentecostal–fundamentalist evangelism calls for comment. This is the emphasis on all means of mass communication — books, tapes, videos. Global Literature Lifeline runs a thoroughly fundamentalist correspondence course which at any one time caters for 10 000 people in Zimbabwe. This body also publishes seven of Gordon Lindsay's publications, some subsidized by Lindsay's organization, and sends them out with the correspondence course. Lindsay's booklets are classic fundamentalism, and strongly dispensationalist. Consider his six-pamphlet set entitled *Miracles in the Bible*. The fifth of these booklets is called *The Twelve 450-Year Judgement Cycles*. In this, Lindsay works out from the Bible that God brings judgement on the earth every 450 years. He proves this because his understanding of the Old Testament enables him to date the Creation at 4000 BC, the Fall in 3993 BC, Noah's birth in 2959 BC, the Flood in 2367 BC, and so on; subsequent judgements of God are the Black Death in AD 1347, the 'Napoleonic Woe' in AD 1797, and the violence, crime, immorality, divorce and communism, which can be conveniently dated as beginning in AD 1947. According to this reckoning, the last judgement will occur in AD 2997, and the end of the world in AD 3001. *Why the Bible is the Word of God* is equally fundamentalist. Lindsay 'proves' his case that only God could be the author of Scripture by twenty proofs. Proof 11 is that 2600 years ago the Bible said the world was round: 'it is he that sitteth upon the circle of the earth' (Isa. 40: 21ff.). Proof 16 is that the Bible predicted the invention of television: the Bible talks of the Antichrist's killing the prophets of God, and their dead bodies being left in the street for three and a half days, and 'peoples and tongues and nations shall see their dead bodies for three days and a half' (Rev. 11: 9) — how could that be possible without television? Proof 17 is that the Bible predicted the age of the motor car: Nahum wrote, 'The chariots blaze with fire of steel on the day of his preparation . . . The chariots rage in confusion in the streets, they run to and fro . . . in the broad ways; they flash with steel — making them appear like torches; they rush (in various directions) like forked lightnings' (Nahum 2: 3ff.). The 'flaming torches' are, according to Lindsay, obviously headlights; the 'raging' is obviously the roar of traffic: 'This prophetic foreview of the automobile is so detailed it can hardly be misunderstood'.[59]

[59] All published by Christ For The Nations, Box 24910, Dallas TX 75224, USA; the quotation is from *Why the Bible is the Word of God*, 19.

This is the kind of Christianity purveyed in Zimbabwe's only locally-produced, mass-consumption, biblical material. Its influence stems not from any intrinsic merits — they are few — but from the fact that the main-line churches do not even bother to compete in this area. The main-line churches do not see this as a priority. They will spend their money on machines, equipment, vehicles, medicines and other necessary things, but not on intellectually reputable Bible courses, or on popularized modern mainstream theology. Such materials exist in profusion overseas, but because of cut-backs in foreign currency allocations, the main-line Christian bookshops have either shut down or changed to selling other kinds of literature. As a result, it would be almost impossible now to find in Harare, outside the University bookshop, a religious book published by SPCK, SCM, Orbis, Oxford University Press, Cambridge University Press, Collins, Darton Longman and Todd, and other publishers of modern theology. By contrast, Word of Life Bookshop remains open and well stocked, because its materials are imported on a 'No Currency Involved' basis — that is, the materials are donated free of charge by American missionaries of the Evangelical Alliance Mission (TEAM) who own the shop. The result is that, on the level of literature, pentecostal–fundamentalist Christianity has won by default. This means that, say, a group of Anglican women who want to run a weekly Bible-study group, will probably be forced, through lack of anything else, to use a fundamentalist study course, often enough embodying the whole agenda of the religious right. This is one way in which the main-line churches are being subtly influenced.

The main-line churches have been affected in another way, through the practice of inviting ministers of these mushrooming new ministries to take Sunday services, and of using such ministries for weekend renewals and other activities. In some cases, the influence has been quite marked. The Anglican Church, for example, traditionally rather high in Rhodesia, has some parishes which have more in common with the Christianity of America's Deep South than with any of the strands of the comprehensive Anglican tradition.

I have raised some of the reasons for the spread of an ideological form of Christianity. The example of Latin America, however, alerts us to the possibility of a further reason. This kind of Christianity has definite political and social effects. In Huntington's words, 'The kind of evangelical Protestantism which is sweeping Central America removes its adherents from social struggle and reform, places the onus on God rather than humans to act, and results in submissive resignation while waiting for Jesus' return to bring about change'.[60] Because of these effects, this Christianity can be used by those with interests to protect. Huntington continues, again about Central America, 'The new Bible institutes and faith missions depended on the largesse of oilmen, industrialists, and plantation owners, who viewed their contributions as investments' — investments against any type of Christianity which would challenge unjust structures or speak for the oppressed.[61] And because of what is at stake, some governments have been involved as well. In Latin America, the role of the United States has been well established. But other countries may also involve themselves. Penny Lernoux has shown that as West German interests develop, German agencies have become involved.[62] And there are high-level Japanese links with Moon, for example; his struggle, if not exactly theirs, certainly safeguards Japan's interests.[63] Southern and Central Africa would be foolish not to learn from the experience of Latin America.

Because of their socio-political role, there have been calls to restrict the activities of some of these pentecostal–fundamentalist churches in Zimbabwe. The ZCC has expressed its concern about some of them, questioning, among other things, their sources of income, their insistence on expatriate leadership, their hindering local efforts to develop self-actualization, and, above all, their political stance.[64] The Zimbabwe *Herald* has called for 'concrete measures to protect our people from the machinations of these religious groups'.[65] After the publication of Mahoney's article against Zimbabwe, it went further, calling on 'church organizations themselves . . . [to fight] all the attempts to use the name of God to further imperialist designs which aim at nothing but the re-enslavement of black peoples'.[66] The *Zimbabwe News*, the official magazine of ZANU (PF), stated in an editorial:

Zimbabwe has been 'invaded' by some American-based religious and revivalist organizations that have political rather than spiritual objectives. They are funded

[60] Huntington, 'The prophet motive', 4.
[61] Ibid., 7.
[62] Lernoux, *Cry of the People*, 304–10.
[63] Clarkson, 'Moon's Law', 36–7, 43–4.
[64] *Sunday Mail* (17 Nov, 1985), 1.
[65] *Herald* (18 Nov. 1985), 4.
[66] *Herald* (20 Mar. 1987), 8; the title of the editorial was 'Devil's crusader'.

by well-known right and racist Church organizations in the USA. Their declared purpose is to oppose our Government's policies and not to preach the gospel . . . These religious groups should be scrutinized carefully, and where necessary told that their work is not needed in Zimbabwe.[67]

The government, however, has not moved against these religious groups, with the exception of Moon's Unification Church. Former President, the Revd Canaan Banana, the Hon. Simon Muzenda, then Deputy Prime Minister, and the Hon. Nathan Shamuyarira, then Minister of Information, Posts and Telecommunications, have all acknowledged the problem. They have said that if missionaries were found to be on the 'pay-list of South Africa' or 'working with Renamo', the government would act; but the government will uphold Zimbabwe's constitution which guarantees religious liberty.[68] It is to be hoped that the government will persist in this course, whatever the provocation. Nothing would be gained by banning religious groups of the fundamentalist kind, except to enable Jerry Falwell to say, 'I told you so'. (In 1980, Falwell praised the apartheid regime in South Africa for its 'support of religious freedom', and then attacked 'Comrade Mugabe, the new Marxist dictator', suggesting that he would suppress Christian freedom in Zimbabwe.)[69] It must be accepted that at times and in places of great social change revivalist movements will spread. The government could do something by giving a greater priority, in allocating foreign currency, to popular presentations of modern main-line Christianity. Christianity is a significant force in the lives of a good part of the population, and current main-line theology could contribute more in the long run to sustained social development than quite a few tractors. However, this is really a matter for Christians themselves. The main-line churches must take seriously their duty to understand the social role religion inevitably plays, and should educate their members on this issue. Then they can ensure that Christianity is in the business of saving people, in all senses. This is in Christianity's own interest. Any other kind of Christianity is a perversion which discredits all Christians.

[67] *Zimbabwe News* (Oct. 1987), 2.
[68] See Askin, 'Is religious freedom misused?', 9–10.
[69] Discussed in Fitzgerald, *Cities on a Hill*, 171.

Select
Bibliography

AGEE, P. *Inside the Company: CIA Diary* (New York, Bantam, 1976).

AMIS, M. *The Moronic Inferno and Other Visits to America* (London, Cape, 1986).

ASKIN, S. 'Hostility, conflict engulf World Vision', *National Catholic Reporter* (23 Apr. 1982), 9–11, 35–6.

ASKIN, S. 'Is religious freedom misused in Zimbabwe?', *Moto* (Oct. 1987), 9–10.

AULÉN, G. *Christus Victor: An Historical Study of the Three Main Types of the Idea of the Atonement* (New York, Macmillan, 1969 [German original, 1930]).

BANKS, A. S. (ed.) *Political Handbook of the World, 1984–85* (Binghamton NY, CSA Publications, 1985).

BARR, J. *Escaping from Fundamentalism* (London, SCM, 1984).

BARR, J. *Fundamentalism* (London, SCM, 1977).

BARR, J. 'The fundamentalist understanding of Scripture', in H. Küng and J. Moltmann (eds.), *Conflicting Ways of Interpreting the Bible* (Edinburgh, T. & T. Clark, *Concilium* 138, No. 8, 1980), 70–4.

BARR, J. 'The problem of fundamentalism today', in J. Barr (ed.), *Explorations in Theology, 7* (London, SCM, 1980), 65–90.

BARRY, T., PREUSCH, D. and SIMS, B. *The New Right Humanitarians* (Albuquerque, The Inter-Hemispheric Education Resource Center, 1986).

BAUM, G. *Religion and Alienation* (New York, Paulist Press, 1975).

BEESON, T. and PEARCE, J. *A Vision of Hope* (London, Collins, 1984).

BELLAH, R. N. *Beyond Belief: Essays on Religion in a Post-Traditional World* (New York, Harper and Row, 1976).

BELLAH, R. N. and HAMMOND, P. E. *Varieties of Civil Religion* (San Francisco, Harper and Row, 1980).

BERGER, B. and BERGER P. L. 'Our conservatism and theirs', *Commentary* (Oct. 1986), 62–7.

BERGER, P. L. *An Invitation to Sociology: A Humanistic Perspective* (Harmondsworth, Penguin, 1966).

BERGER, P. L. *A Rumour of Angels: Modern Society and the Rediscovery of the Supernatural* (Harmondsworth, Penguin, 1970).

BERGER, P. L. *The Sacred Canopy: Elements of a Sociological Theory of Religion* (New York, Doubleday, 1967).

BERGER, P. L. and LUCKMANN, T. *The Social Construction of Reality* (Harmondsworth, Penguin, 1967).

BIBBY, R. W. 'Why conservative churches *really* are growing: Kelley revisited', *Journal for the Scientific Study of Religion* (1978), XVII, 129–37.

BOFF, L. *Church, Charisma, Power: Liberation Theology and the Institutional Church* (New York, Crossroad, 1985).

BOURGAULT, L. 'The "PTL Club" and Protestant viewers: An ethnographic study', *Journal of Communication* (1985), XXXV, 132–48.

BOYER, J-F. *L'Empire Moon* (Paris, La Découverte, 1986).

BRIGHT, B. *Revolution now* (San Bernardino CA, Campus Crusade, 1969).

BROWN, C. G. 'Fundamentalism: Survival and revival: A review of the literature', *Australian Journal of American Studies* (1987), VI, ii, 34–41.

BROWN, P. *Augustine of Hippo* (London, Faber, 1967).

BROWN, R. E. *Biblical Reflections on Crises Facing the Church* (London, Darton, Longman and Todd, 1975).

BROWN, R. McA. 'Listen, Jerry Falwell!', *Christianity and Crisis* (22 Dec. 1980), 360–4.

BROWN, R. McA. 'The need for a moral minority', *Face to Face* (Winter 1981), VIII, 12–14.

BROWN, R. McA. *Theology in a New Key: Responding to Liberation Themes* (Philadelphia, Westminister Press, 1978).

BUCHANAN, J. 'Church and State: Anatomy of a relationship', *CALC Report [Unmasking the Religious Right]* (1987), XIII, iii–iv, 18–28.

CABESTRERO, T. *Ministers of God, Ministers of the People: Testimonies of Faith from Nicaragua* (Maryknoll NY, Orbis, 1983 [Spanish original, 1982]).

CARDENAL, E. *The Gospel in Solentiname* (Maryknoll NY, Orbis, 4 vols., 1976–82).

CHADWICK, O. *The Secularization of the European Mind in the Nineteenth Century* (Cambridge, Cambridge Univ. Press, 1975).

CHAPPLE, S. 'Whole lotta savin' goin' on: The gospel according to Jimmy Lee Swaggart', *Mother Jones* (July–Aug. 1986), 37–45, 86.

CHERRY, C. *God's New Israel: Religious Interpretations of American Destiny* (Englewood Cliffs, Prentice-Hall, 1974).

CLARKSON, F. 'Moon's law: God is phasing out democracy', *Covert Action Information Bulletin* (Spring 1987), 36–46.

COHN, N. *The Pursuit of the Millennium: Revolutionary Millenarians and Mystical Anarchists of the Middle Ages* (London, Paladin, 1970 [original, 1957]).

COMMITTEE OF SANTA FE. *A New Inter-American Policy for the Eighties* (Washington, Council for Inter-American Security, 1980).

CONGREGATION FOR THE DOCTRINE OF THE FAITH. *Christian Freedom and Liberation* (Vatican City, The Congregation, 1986).

CONGREGATION FOR THE DOCTRINE OF THE FAITH. *Instructions on Some Aspects of the Theology of Liberation* (Vatican City, The Congregation, 1984).

DANIÉLOU, J., COURATIN, A. H. and KENT, J. *Historical Theology* (Harmondsworth, Penguin, Pelican Guide to Modern Theology 2, 1969).

DE HAAS, M. 'Is millenarianism alive and well in White South Africa?', *Religion in Southern Africa* (1986), VII, 37–45.

DE KLERK, W. A. *The Puritans in Africa: A Story of Afrikanerdom* (Harmondsworth, Penguin, 1976).

DIAMOND, S. 'Shepherding', *Covert Action Information Bulletin* (Spring 1987), 18–31.

DIDION, J. 'Washington in Miami', *New York Review of Books* (16 July 1987), 22–31.

DOMINGUEZ, E. 'The great commission', *Nacla Report on the Americas* (Jan.–Feb. 1984), (XVIII), 12–22.

DUGGER, R. 'Reagan's Apocalypse Now', *Guardian* (21 Apr. 1984), 19.

DULLES, A. *Models of the Church* (New York, Doubleday, 1974).

EASTERBROOK, G. 'Ideas move nations: How conservative think tanks have helped to transform the forms of political debate', *Atlantic Monthly* (Jan. 1986), CCLVII, vii, 66–80.

ECUMENICAL RESEARCH UNIT. *Throw Yourself Down: A Consideration of the Main Teachings of the Prosperity Cults* (Pretoria, The Unit, n.d.).

Evangelical Witness in South Africa: A Critique of Evangelical Theology and Practice by Evangelicals Themselves (Dobsonville, South Africa, 'Concerned Evangelicals', 1986).

FALWELL, J. *Listen, America!* (New York, Doubleday, 1980).

FIERRO, A. *The Militant Gospel: An Analysis of Contemporary Political Theologies* (London, SCM, 1977 [Spanish original, 1975]).

FITZGERALD, F. *Cities on a Hill: A Journey through Contemporary American Culture* (London, Picador, 1987).

FREDERIKSE, J. *None but Ourselves: Masses vs. Media in the Making of Zimbabwe* (Harare, Zimbabwe Publishing House, 1982).

GARDNER, M. 'Giving God a hand', *New York Review of Books* (13 Aug. 1987), 17–23.

GIFFORD, P. ' "Africa shall be saved": An appraisal of Reinhard Bonnke's pan-African crusade', *Journal of Religion in Africa* (1987), XVII, 63–92.

GREEN, P. 'Holy matrimony: The church right and apartheid', *Weekly Mail* (8–14 Apr. 1988), 8–9.

GUTH, J. L. 'The new Christian right', in R. C. Liebman and R. Wuthnow (eds.), *The New Christian Right: Mobilization and Legitimation* (New York, Aldine, 1983), 31–48.

GUTIÉRREZ, G. *A Theology of Liberation* (Maryknoll NY, Orbis, 1973 [Spanish original, 1971]).

HALSELL, G. *Prophecy and Politics: Militant Evangelists on the Road to Nuclear War* (New York, Lawrence Hill, 1987).

HAMILTON, M. 'Churches aiding destabilization in Southern Africa', *Herald* (13 Jan. 1988), 4.

HASTINGS, A. *A History of African Christianity 1950–1975* (Cambridge, Cambridge Univ. Press, 1979).

HASTINGS, A. *A History of English Christianity 1920–85* (London, Collins, 1986).

HASTINGS, A. *Wiriyamu* (London, Search Press, 1974).

HERBERG, W. *Protestant–Catholic–Jew: An Essay in American Religious Sociology* (New York, Doubleday, rev. edn., 1960).

HIMMELSTEIN, J. L. 'The New Right', in R. C. Liebman and R. Wuthnow (eds.), *The New Christian Right: Mobilization and Legitimation* (New York, Aldine, 1983), 13–30.

HOLLENWEGER, W. J. *The Pentecostals* (London, SCM, 1972 [German original, 1969]).

HORSFIELD, P. G. *Religious Television: The American Experience* (New York, Longman, 1984).

HOULDEN, J. L. *Connections* (London, SCM, 1986).

HOULDEN, J. L. *Patterns of Faith: A Study in the Relationship between the New Testament and Christian Doctrine* (London, SCM, 1977).

HUNT, D. *Beyond Seduction: A Return to Biblical Christianity* (Eugene OR, Harvest House, 1987).

HUNTINGTON, D. 'God's saving plan', *Nacla Report on the Americas* (Jan.–Feb. 1984), XVIII, 23–36.

HUNTINGTON, D. 'The prophet motive', *Nacla Report on the Americas* (Jan.–Feb. 1984), XVIII, 2–11.

JACKSON, G. 'South Africa's new evangelicals: A new movement with new answers', *To the Point* (2 June 1978), 20–2.

JOHNSON, R. W. 'Rising Moon', *London Review of Books* (18 Dec. 1986) 3–6.

JOINT WORKING COMMITTEE OF THE N[ATIONAL] C[OUNCIL OF] C[HURCHES]/ R[OMAN] C[ATHOLIC] C[HURCH], *The Church and Fundamentalism* (Christchurch, New Zealand, The Committee, Thirty-first report, [1984]).

JONES, L. 'Reagan's religion', *Journal of American Culture* (1985), VIII, 59–70.

JONES, L. 'Right-wing evangelicals and South Africa', *Moto* (Apr. 1988), 12–13.

JORSTAD, E. *The Politics of Moralism: The New Christian Right in American Life* (Minneapolis, Augsburg Publishing House, 1981).

Kairos Document: Challenge to the Church: A Theological Comment on the Political Crisis in South Africa (Braamfontein, Transvaal, The Kairos Theologians, [1985]).

KATER, J. L. *Christians on the Right: The Moral Majority in Perspective* (New York, Scabury Press, 1982).

KELLEY, D. M. 'Why conservative churches are still growing', *Journal for the Scientific Study of Religion* (1978), XVII, 165–72.

KICKHAM, L. 'Holy Spirit or Holy Spook?', *Covert Action Information Bulletin* (Spring 1987), 4–8.

KICKHAM, L. 'The theology of nuclear war', *Covert Action Information Bulletin* (Spring 1987), 9–17.

KNOX, R. *Enthusiasm: A Chapter in the History of Religion, with Special Reference to the XVII and XVIII Centuries* (Oxford, Oxford Univ. Press, 1962).

KÜNG, H. *On Being a Christian* (London, Collins, 1978 [German original, 1974]).

LAHAYE, T. *Faith of Our Founding Fathers* (Brentwood TN, Wolgemuth and Hyatt, 1987).

LANG, A. 'Armageddon theology', *CALC Report [Unmasking the Religious Right]* (1987), XIII, iii–iv, 5–17.

LANG, A. 'The emergence of a phenomenon called the religious right', *CALC Report [Unmasking the Religious Right]* (1987), XIII, iii–iv, 29–38.

LAPSLEY, M. *Neutrality or Co-option? Anglican Church and State from 1964 until the Independence of Zimbabwe* (Gweru, Mambo Press, 1986).

LASH, N. *Change in Focus: A Study of Doctrinal Change and Continuity* (London, Sheed and Ward, 1973).

LERNOUX, P. *Cry of the People: The Struggle for Human Rights in Latin America: The Catholic Church in Conflict with US Policy* (New York, Penguin, 2nd edn, 1982).

LEWIS, N. *The Missionaries* (London, Secker, 1988).

LINDEN, I. *The Catholic Church and the Struggle for Zimbabwe* (London, Longman, 1980).

LINDSEY, H. with CARLSON, C. C. *The Late Great Planet Earth* (New York, Bantam, 1970).

MACEOIN, G. and RILEY, N. *Puebla: A Church Being Born* (New York, Paulist Press, 1980).

MCLOUGHLIN, W. G. and BELLAH, R. N. (eds.) *Religion in America* (Boston, Beacon Press, 1968).

MCSWEENEY, B. *Roman Catholicism: The Search for Relevance* (Oxford, Blackwell, 1980).

MAGUIRE, D. *The New Subversives: The Anti-Americanism of the Religious Right* (New York, Continuum, 1982).

MARSDEN, G. M. *Fundamentalism and American Culture: The Shaping of Twentieth-Century Evangelicalism, 1870–1925* (New York, Oxford Univ. Press, 1980).

MARTIN, D. and JOHNSON, P. *The Struggle for Zimbabwe* (Harare, Zimbabwe Publishing House, 1981).

115

MEREDITH, M. *The Past is Another Country: Rhodesia 1890–1979* (London, Deutsch, 1979).

MICHELL, J. *Church Ablaze: The Hatfield Baptist Church Story* (Basingstoke, Hants, Marshall Pickering, 1985).

MORRAN, E. S. and SCHLEMMER, L. *Faith for the Fearful? An Investigation into New Churches in the Greater Durban Area* (Durban, University of Natal, Centre for Applied Social Sciences, 1984).

NILSSON, F. *Parakyrkligt: Om Business och Bön i Sverige* (Stockholm, Verbum, 1988).

NOTH, M. *Exodus* (Philadelphia, Westminster Press, 1962 [German original, 1959]).

O'BRIEN, C. C. 'God and man in Nicaragua', *Atlantic Monthly* (Aug. 1986), CCLVIII, ii, 50–72.

O'BRIEN, M. 'The Christian underground', *Covert Action Information Bulletin* (Spring 1987), 32–5.

PELIKAN, J. *Jesus through the Centuries: His Place in the History of Culture* (New Haven, Yale Univ. Press, 1985).

PELL, E. *The Big Chill* (Boston, Beacon Press, 1984).

QUEBEDEAUX, R. *I Found It: The Story of Bill Bright and Campus Crusade* (London, Hodder, 1980).

RICHARDSON, A. 'The rise of modern biblical scholarship and recent discussion of the authority of the Bible', in S. L. Greenslade (ed.), *Cambridge History of the Bible: III* (Cambridge, Cambridge Univ. Press, 1963), 294–338.

'The rise of the religious right in Central America', *Inter-Hemispheric Education Resource Center Bulletin* [Albuquerque] (Summer–Fall 1987).

ROBERTSON, P. *Answers to Two Hundred of Life's Most Probing Questions* (New York, Nelson, 1984).

ROBERTSON, P. and BUCKINGHAM, J. *Shout It from the Housetops: The Story of the Founder of the Christian Broadcasting Network* (New York, Bridge Publications, 1972).

ROBERTSON, P. with SLOSSER, B. *The Secret Kingdom: A Promise of Hope and Freedom in a World of Turmoil* (New York, Bantam, 1984 [original, 1982]).

RUSHDIE, S. *The Jaguar Smile: A Nicaraguan Journey* (London, Picador, 1987).

SAMPSON, A. *Black and Gold: Tycoons, Revolutionaries and Apartheid* (London, Coronet, 1987).

SCHOOF, T. M. *A Survey of Catholic Theology 1800–1970* (New York, Paulist-Newman Press, 1970).

SECRETARIAT FOR PROMOTING CHRISTIAN UNITY *Report on Sects, Cults and New Religious Movements* (Vatican City, The Secretariat, 1986).

SHAKARIAN, D. as told to J. and E. Sherrill. *The Happiest People on Earth: The Long-awaited Personal Story of Demos Shakarian* (Old Tappan NJ, Spire Books, 1975).

SHEPARD, W. ' "Fundamentalism": Christian and Islamic', *Religion* (1987), XVII, 355–78.

SHRIVER, P. L. *The Bible Vote: Religion and the New Right* (New York, Pilgrim Press, 1981).

SIMPSON, J. H. 'Moral issues and status politics', in R. C. Liebman and R. Wuthnow (eds.), *The New Christian Right: Mobilization and Legitimation* (New York, Aldine, 1983), 187–205.

SOUTH AFRICA. *Report of the Commission of Inquiry into the Mass Media* [Chairman: M. T. Steyn] (Pretoria, Govt. Printer, RP 89/1981).

SOUTH AFRICA. *Report of the Commission of Inquiry into the South African Council of Churches* [Chairman: C. F. Eloff] (Pretoria, Govt. Printer, RP 74/1983).

STEELE, R. *Plundering Hell: The Reinhard Bonnke Story* (Ravenmoor, South Africa, Sceptre Publications, 1984).

SYKES, S. *The Identity of Christianity* (London, SPCK, 1984).

UNITED STATES. Department of State. 'Quality of life in the Americas: Report of a US Presidential Mission for the Western hemisphere' [Rockefeller Mission Report], *Department of State Bulletin* (1969), LXI, 493–540.

VALDERREY, J. 'Sects in Central America: A pastoral problem', *Pro Mundi Vita Bulletin* (1985), C.

VERRYN, T. *Rich Christian, Poor Christian: An Appraisal of Rhema Teachings* (Pretoria, Ecumenical Research Unit, 1983).

VIDAL, G. *Armageddon? Essays, 1983–1987* (London, Deutsch, 1987).

VILLA-VICENCIO, C. 'Theology in the service of the State: The Steyn and Eloff Commissions', in C. Villa-Vicencio and J. W. de Gruchy (eds.), *Resistance and Hope: South African Essays in Honour of Beyers Naudé* (Cape Town, D. Philip, 1985), 112–25.

WALLIS, J. and MICHAELSON, W. 'The plan to save America', *Sojourners* (Apr. 1976), 3–12.

WEYRICH, P. M. 'Blue collar or blue blood? The New Right compared with the old right', in R. W. Whitaker (ed.), *The New Right Papers* (New York, St Martin's Press, 1982), 48–62.

WOODWARD, B. *Veil: The Secret Wars of the CIA, 1981–1987* (London, Simon and Schuster, 1987).

WORLD VISION INTERNATIONAL *Understanding Who We Are* (Monrovia CA, World Vision International, n.d.).

ZACHRISSON, P. *An African Area in Change: Belingwe 1894–1946: A Study of Colonialism, Missionary Activity and African Response in Southern Rhodesia* (Gothenburg, Univ. of Gothenburg Press, 1978).

NEWSPAPERS AND MAGAZINES

Accent	Wellington, New Zealand
African Voice	Pietermaritzburg
Atlantic Monthly	Boston
Commentary	New York
Covert Action Information Bulletin	Washington DC
Guardian	London
Guardian Weekly	Manchester
Herald	Harare
International Herald Tribune	Paris
Le Monde	Paris
London Review of Books	London
Los Angeles Times	Los Angeles
Monthly Letter on Evangelism	Geneva
Mother Jones	San Francisco
Moto	Gweru
National Catholic Reporter	Kansas City
New York Review of Books	New York
New York Times	New York
Newsweek	New York
Observer	London
Orange County Register	California
Plain Truth	Pasadena CA
San Diego Magazine	San Diego
San Francisco Chronicle	San Francisco
Sojourners	Washington DC
Sunday Mail	Harare
Sunday Tribune	Durban
Tablet	London
The Economist	London
The Month	London
The Times	London
Time	New York
To the Point	Johannesburg
Voice	Costa Mesa CA
Weekly Mail	Johannesburg
Zimbabwe News	Harare